The BUTCHER Babe™ COOKBOOK

The BUTCHER Babe™ COOKBOOK

Comfort Food Hacked by a Classically Trained Chef

Loreal Gavin

Celebrity Chef and winner of *Cutthroat Kitchen*

PAGE STREET
PUBLISHING CO.

PAGE STREET
PUBLISHING CO.

First published in 2017 by
Page Street Publishing Co.
27 Congress Street, Suite 105
Salem, MA 01970
www.pagestreetpublishing.com

Distributed by Macmillan, sales in Canada by The Canadian Manda Group.

20 19 18 17   1 2 3 4

ISBN-13: 978-1-62414-327-4
ISBN-10: 1-62414-327-X

Library of Congress Control Number: 2016954579

Cover and book design by Page Street Publishing Co.
Photography by Jessica Ebelhar

Printed and bound in China

Page Street is proud to be a member of 1% for the Planet. Members donate one percent of their sales to one or more of the over 1,500 environmental and sustainability charities across the globe who participate in this program.

This book is dedicated to
MY GRANDMOTHER, SUSIE GAVIN.

✳ ✦ ✳

Contents

FOREWORD

Loreal's love for cooking was made quite evident to me when she was only 4 or 5 years of age. One of her most favorite things to do as a child was to watch me cook. She would push a kitchen stool up to my cabinets, and would want to help with anything and everything I was preparing for our meals. "Grandma, let me stir" or "Grandma, let me roll the dough."

She wanted to learn how to prepare steaks (which she called "the meat with lines on it"), because her grandfather told her it should become one of her favorite foods to make her big and strong.

The years passed. I shared my cooking and baking skills with her, and after graduating from high school, she decided to pursue her dream of becoming a chef. She moved to Louisville, Kentucky to become a student of culinary arts.

Because I came from a farm family of 11 children, I taught Loreal the importance of making much from little. Our food consisted of animals, a large garden and an even bigger truck patch where my parents planted potatoes, navy beans, melons and cantaloupe. We also had an orchard with all kinds of fruit trees, including grape vines, strawberries and raspberries.

Food was plentiful but never wasted. Loreal learned from me that you don't throw away good food, because another meal can always be made from leftovers by adding some new ingredients.

Perhaps this explains why when she was a little girl she told her friends "my grandma is a scratch cooker."

It really amazes me that she has the ability to add a few new things, then a little bit of 'this and that' to make some of my old traditional family recipes more savory—a completely new taste.

I am proud of her and all her accomplishments, and hope you enjoy the recipes as much as she enjoyed sharing them with you.

As for me, I will always think of her when I have good things to eat, and continue to tell the story of my granddaughter—"The Butcher Babe."

—Susie Gavin

NICE TO MEAT YOU
A Meat Manifesto by the Butcher Babe

In my grandma's old country house, I was introduced to an ingredient that she knew deep in her bones. This ingredient is a part of every dish she creates. This uncanny flavor lingers on your lips for years. I've seen many cooks make beautiful dishes, but forget to add this one important component. You can't buy this ingredient at the grocery store or grow it out in the garden, because it lives within you.

This ingredient is love. This cookbook and the recipes I've created to share with you encompass the values and flavors from a "more simple time" with Southern flare. You often hear the saying, "They don't make things like they used to." Such can be said for lots of recipes floating out there in the world.

My childhood memories revolve around the garden posts where my bare feet grew deep roots. As a little girl in Louisiana, I loved playing in the dirt and my curious nature sprouted wild like weeds while I grew like one. I didn't grow up with much, but I sure as hell never went hungry.

Growing up, I never really left the garden. My first job was detasseling corn. If you don't know what that is, then consider yourself lucky. The only thing I earned that summer was a nice farmer's tan under the hot Indiana sun and respect for the blue-collar condition.

Luckily, I'm not a stranger to hard work so I began doing dishes in a restaurant. At 15 years young, I started finding little pieces of myself in every laborious task I met. It felt good bringing smiles to the faces of people I'd never meet. My glamorous life as a "line cook" had begun, and before I knew it the chef life completely swept me off my feet. Cooking was my first love, and let me tell you, I fell fast and hard.

After years of working in the Midwest, I found myself bored of cooking for racecar teams and master distillers. So, I started to work in a family-owned butcher shop. The butcher shop life felt like home to me, and I was proud to have the experience as a cornerstone of my education. Let's be real here, I also did it for the steaks.

My Southern roots were having a hard time flourishing in the cold, harsh winters of Indiana. Eventually my gypsy spirit started tugging at my sleeve for something new. I sold or gave away everything I owned except for my guitar and my dirt bike. I took a one-way, solo train ride out to "the Bay" in California. My family and I couldn't tell if I was crazy or brilliant.

I found myself struggling to live the American dream within the walls of a hostel on Telegraph Avenue. As a last resort before calling home crying, I tried out for a show on Food Network as a joke. They liked me, no, they loved me, or at least Alton Brown did. I ended up almost winning the *Next Food Network Star*. I found myself under the bright lights of television.

Behind white knuckles and some red lipstick, "The Butcher Babe" was born. I went on to win *Cutthroat Kitchen*. Who knew this little country bumpkin would end up cooking on television, headlining food shows nationally and writing a cookbook! I owe all my success to my country roots, good soil, music, motorcycles, art, faith and lil' salt 'n' pepper. A great red lipstick never hurt either.

I invite you to spend time with this book. Let its stories and flavors inspire you to create your own recipes and share them with the ones you love. Smile with your eyes and cook with your heart.

xoxo

Chapter 1

HAVE YOUR STEAK AND EAT IT TOO:
～ Beef ～

Back in the day, I used to try to cook all my barbecue on the grill, only to realize after several burnt pieces of pre-sauced meat that they were just burning to death. If you're going to sauce your meat, do it after it's done cooking and then finish it on the grill. That's the key to success there, guys. Also, start off with a nice and clean grill. I like to use an old rolled-up towel that's been doused in oil. I'll take a pair of tongs and quickly run it over the grates of the grill after a good brushing.

Shop the clearance section for great beef finds. If it's got some darkened exterior, I want it! The age just adds to the flavor. What do you think dry aging is? Dry aging is basically just a steak hanging in a refrigerator for around 30 days or more. The effect of constant refrigeration adds to the overall flavor profile of the beef, resulting in a more tender, flavorful steak. Beef is the only raw meat I'll buy from the clearance section. So think again next time you see that lonely browned pack of ribeyes at the grocery store. With all the savings, you can go buy some bourbon.

One-Pot Wonders
Buttermilk Beef Stroganoff and Buttermilk Biscuits — 15
Pork Bolognese with Grit Cake and Gremolata — 19
Sunday Chuck Roast with Grandma's Secret Sauce — 21
Liver and Onions and Celery Root Mash with Bacon Gravy — 22
Drunken Shanks with Root Puree — 24

Barbecue
Barbecue Brisket and Collards with Peach Barbecue Sauce — 27
East-Meets-South Short Ribs with Fig Glaze
and Cilantro Pesto — 29

Whole Roasts
Lunch Box Roast Beef with Horseradish Cream — 30
Thyme-Crusted Ribeye Roast with Apricot Mustard — 32
Whole Beef Tenderloin with Green and Pink Peppercorn Rub — 33

Steaks
Filet with Bourbon Blue Cheese Sauce — 35
Hoosier Ribeye with Vidalia Onion Chutney — 36
Porterhouse with Pan Sauce — 39
Southern-Fried Steak with Pecan Butter — 41
Beef Tongue Tacos — 42

Grinds
Pimento Burger — 45
Meat Loaf with Tomato Jam — 47
Steak Tartare in Avocado Bowls — 48

BUTTERMILK BEEF STROGANOFF
and BUTTERMILK BISCUITS

When I hear the word "buttermilk," my mouth waters. Buttermilk has a flavor that is slightly tangy, very similar to sour cream. Beef Stroganoff is usually paired with pasta, but in this recipe I found an excuse to make biscuits instead! With the addition of fresh dill, seared mushrooms and caramelized beef, before you know it you've made a quick meal that will "stick to your ribs," as grandma would say. I think if buttermilk biscuits and pasta got in a fight, I'm pretty sure that buttermilk biscuits would win. To be completely honest, if I'm filling up on any carbs it better be some flaky biscuits. You can't eat jelly on some pasta! One time I ate 8 buttermilk biscuits with an entire jar of honey, but that's another story.

SERVES 8

2 lb (900 g) top sirloin, flank, skirt, round, strip, ribeye or filet

1½ tbsp (23 g) freshly cracked black pepper

1½ tbsp (23 g) salt

1 tsp sugar

1 tbsp (8 g) garlic powder

1 tbsp (8 g) smoked paprika

½ cup (76 g) cornstarch

½ cup (120 ml) vegetable oil

1 lb (455 g) baby portabella, shiitake or white button mushrooms, sliced

2 tbsp (28 g) butter

8 cups (1.9 L) cold beef stock, divided

¼ cup (60 ml) brandy

BUTTERMILK BISCUITS

3 tsp (11 g) baking powder

½ tsp baking soda

½ tsp salt

2 cups (500 g) all-purpose flour

4 tbsp (56 g) butter or shortening

Ice cubes, as needed

1 cup (250 ml) buttermilk

Cut the meat against the grain into bite-size pieces. Combine the pepper, salt, sugar, garlic powder, smoked paprika and cornstarch in a bowl and toss the meat in the spice mixture.

To make the biscuits, sift together the baking powder, baking soda, salt and flour and set the mixture aside in the freezer if possible. For this recipe, I like to use butter rather than shortening. I put the butter in the freezer until it is frozen solid. The trick in getting a buttery, flaky crust is maintaining those pretty little flecks of butter during the mixing process.

Using a potato peeler, you will essentially peel the butter. I peel mine right over the dry ingredients. Lightly toss the flecks of butter in the flour mixture and let it set in the freezer or fridge for about 10 minutes. At this point, preheat the oven to 350°F (177°C).

While the flour mixture is chilling, drop a couple ice cubes in the buttermilk. You can use a fork to keep them out of your forming dough. The purpose of the cubes isn't to dilute the buttermilk but to chill it.

Slowly pour the buttermilk into the chilled flour mixture. I like to use the same fork to gently incorporate the two. Don't forget to scrape the sides of the bowl while also not overmixing. Roll out dough and use a glass to cut round biscuit shapes. Place on a baking sheet and bake the biscuits for about 10 to 12 minutes until they are golden brown.

In a large, heavy-bottomed pan, add the vegetable oil and bring it to medium-high heat. Before I sear the meat in the pan, I like to sprinkle a bit of flour into the vegetable oil once it's coming up to temperature in order to tell how hot it is. If the flour starts to sizzle a little bit, that's a sign that you're good to go. If the oil is smoking, that's a sign it's way too hot.

I use vegetable oil for this because it has a higher smoke point compared to olive oil. If an oil becomes too hot, it will burn and develop an unwanted flavor. If this happens to you, just toss the oil and start over. I've burned a million things in my lifetime.

(continued)

BUTTERMILK BEEF STROGANOFF *and* BUTTERMILK BISCUITS *(continued)*

Once the pan and oil are at a perfect searing temperature, evenly distribute the coated meat pieces in the pan. You should hear a nice searing noise as this occurs. The next trick involves not trying to loosen the meat from the bottom of the pan.

Let the meat hang out for a few minutes and let a nice crust form before you try to give it a toss. The Maillard reaction is taking place as it caramelizes the natural carbohydrates found in the meat. The Maillard reaction also occurs in breads as amino acids give browned foods a desired flavor.

After you remove the meat morsels from the bottom of the pan, place them to the side to add back to the sauce later. (You don't want them to overcook and become dry or tough.) Next, add the mushrooms and butter to the pan. Give them a nice stir with the meat drippings and let them caramelize for about 5 minutes on medium heat.

After 10 minutes of browning, turn off the heat and, with a wooden spoon, start to slowly incorporate the cold beef stock, adding 1 cup (240 ml) at a time and gently stirring after each addition. Add the brandy and stir until incorporated. Bring the stroganoff to a simmer, but do not boil. Add the meat back to the pan to cover in the sauce.

Serve beef stroganoff over buttermilk biscuits.

Butcher Babe Tips

✳ Did you know you can make your own buttermilk at home? All it takes is milk and an acid, such as lemon juice. The ratio is easy to remember: 1 tablespoon (15 ml) acid per 1 cup (240 ml) milk = 1 cup (240 ml) buttermilk. So, for example, if you need 3 cups (720 ml) buttermilk, simply add 3 tablespoons (45 ml) lemon juice to 3 cups (720 ml) milk, and you have instant homemade buttermilk!

✳ While you're at it, you might as well double the biscuit recipe so that you can freeze half the dough. There's nothing wrong with having some biscuits lying around. I go ahead and roll mine out as the recipe recommends and freeze them on a tray for about an hour. Once they have become 'individually frozen,' I pop them into an airtight plastic bag or container. They will last in the freezer for up to 3 months. Follow the same baking instructions.

WHAT DOES "THE GRAIN" MEAN WHEN WE ARE TALKING ABOUT MEAT, AND HOW CAN I CUT AGAINST IT?

Meat is made up of groups of muscle fibers that run very closely to one another, also known as striations. One must be able to see and understand the various ways in which these muscular groups run together and how to cut against them. Simply examine the direction in which the meats' fibers are running, then cut in the opposite direction. The time you want to cut with the grain is when making Beef Jerky (page 118). Why? Because you want a tough, chewy snack!

PORK BOLOGNESE *with* GRIT CAKE AND GREMOLATA

Bolognese is one of those dishes you just can't be mad at. It's like the best tomato soup you've ever had bought a one-way ticket to Italy and made a beeline for the butcher shop once it got there. Speaking of making a trip to the butcher shop, this recipe walks you through the simple steps of making your own Italian-flavored sausage in your own home. You'll discover how easy it is to infuse custom grinds at home with the types of flavors you love, like crushed red pepper, sage and oregano.

Get ready to fill your house with notes of garlic and red wine simmering with one another. Its comforting flavors make you feel right at home. I like it even better on day two or three, when all the flavors have had a chance to really marry with one another.

SERVES 8

1½ lb (683 g) ground pork

1½ lb (683) ground beef (preferably 80/20; the fattier, the better)

2 tbsp (30 g) sea salt

1 tbsp (15 g) freshly cracked black pepper

1 tbsp (7 g) red chili flakes

1 tbsp (8 g) caraway seeds

2 tsp (4 g) dried sage

2 tbsp (2 g) dried oregano

1 tbsp (1 g) dried thyme

1 tbsp (14 g) packed brown sugar

3 tbsp (45 ml) olive oil

2 cups (360 g) peeled medium dice sweet potatoes

2 cups (300 g) medium dice white onion

2 cups (300 g) medium dice celery

2 cups (300 g) medium dice carrots

4 cups (640 g) medium dice fresh tomatoes (skin and seeds are OK)

3 cups (720 ml) red wine

3 cups (720 ml) cold water

1 cup (240 ml) red wine vinegar

GRIT CAKE

8 cups (1.9 L) water

2 cups (340 g) stone-ground grits (not instant)

Salt and freshly cracked black pepper, to taste

2 tbsp (28 g) butter

1½ lb (683 g) Parmigiano-Reggiano (or any other sharp, melting cheese)

GREMOLATA

1 bunch flat-leaf parsley, cleaned and stems removed

1 whole head garlic, minced

4 lemons, zested

Preheat the oven to 400°F (204°C).

In a large bowl, mix the pork and beef with the salt, pepper, red chili flakes, caraway seeds, sage, oregano, thyme and brown sugar to create your Bolognese meat base. The more you make these sort of grinds, the more comfortable you will become infusing them with your personality and flavor profiles. You can always make the sausage and sear off a small bite to see if you're in the right neighborhood. If not, you can always add more seasoning.

Pour the olive oil into a large, heavy-bottomed, oven-safe 8-quart (7.5-L) pot over medium-high heat. Add the sweet potatoes, onion, celery, carrots, tomatoes, red wine, cold water and red wine vinegar and cook until a little bit of color starts to develop. You may even notice a nice golden-brown color starting to develop on the bottom of the pan.

Add the Bolognese meat mixture and brown it as well. As the meat cooks, you'll notice some golden-brown pieces sticking to the bottom of the pot. This is called fond (pronounced like "fawn"). The best way to remove fond is by deglazing the pot with an acid of some sort. The acid in this case is the wine and tomatoes.

In a heavy-bottomed saucepan, bring the water to a boil. Pour in the grits. Cook the grits for about 20 to 25 minutes on medium heat. Once the grits become nice and soft, season them with salt and pepper. Pour the grits into a medium casserole pan that has been smeared with butter. Let the grits chill in the refrigerator until set, which takes about 45 minutes. I let mine set while I cook the Bolognese. You can skip this step entirely and serve right out of the pan if you're in a pinch for time.

After the grits are set in the pan, I like to use a round circle cutter to remove the portions for my guests. I will transfer them to a baking sheet and bake them for 15 minutes or until hot.

Once the parsley is cleaned and the stems are removed, get ready to chop your heart out. This is a good time to make a lot of noise on your cutting board and start talking with your best Italian accent. We are looking for a pretty fine chop here.

(continued)

Prepare the aromatics and take a step back to admire just how beautiful fresh cut veggies can be.

Grind the meat. Don't you feel like a Renaissance man or woman? Here I'm using the coarse setting for my grinds.

Mix the grinds with the aromatics until well-incorporated.

Sear the Bolognese mixture in the saucepan.

Gremolata can be served as a garnish at room temperature. A few sprinkles of this zesty stuff and your mouth will be watering.

PORK BOLOGNESE *with* GRIT CAKE AND GREMOLATA *(continued)*

Next, let's undress the garlic. Nothing tastes better than fresh garlic and lemon. However, there are some pretty handy garlic peelers out there. So get to peeling and mincing! It's not the most fun job in the world, but it's worth it.

Last but not least, the lemon zest! I love to do this last because the lemon will aid you in removing that garlic smell from your hands. The best tool to use is a rasp grater or a microplane. I went a long time without buying one. I used to use hand graters and potato peelers. I was basically living in a cave.

When you zest citrus fruit (a lemon in this case), take care not to get down to the white pith of the fruit. It is bitter. Really bitter. Save your lemons for cocktails. Duh.

Mix the parsley, garlic and lemon zest together in a small bowl. If stored in an airtight container, this mixture will last 2 days under refrigeration.

Right before I serve the grit cakes, I top them with the Parmigiano-Reggiano and broil them until the cheese becomes golden brown. If you are more into a rustic look, you can also serve the grits hot right out of the pan they were cooked in. I would remind you not to forget the cheese, but you won't. Serve with Pork Bolognese and garnish with gremolata.

SUNDAY CHUCK ROAST
with GRANDMA'S SECRET SAUCE

I've always believed that love is a flavor. My grandmother, Susie Gavin, first introduced that timeless taste to me. I have memories of entering her perfectly tailored home and being comforted by the smell of her magical slow cooker. Every Sunday afternoon, she set her table like it was a national holiday and she'd cook a spread of food that made you swear it was one! I'd be homesick for her company and food, so I'd always try to re-create the dish with no luck! It took me until a few years after culinary school to discover the secrets of this old-school roast. The only reason I know her trick now is because one Christmas, while admiring her cooking, I saw her use it—a packet of Italian dressing seasoning.

SERVES 6

4 whole heads garlic

¼ cup (60 ml) olive oil

Dash salt

1 (3- to 4-lb [1.4- to 1.8-kg]) bone-in or boneless chuck roast (or bone-in or boneless short ribs)

3 tbsp (45 g) kosher salt

3 tbsp (45 g) freshly cracked black pepper

Olive oil, as needed

3 large white onions, large dice

1 lb (455 g) baby carrots

1 bunch celery, roughly chopped (reserve the celery leaves for garnish)

1 lb (455 g) white button mushrooms

2 large tomatoes, large dice (with seeds, skin and juice) or 1 (16-oz [475-ml]) can crushed tomatoes

½ cup (120 ml) red wine

2 cups (480 ml) red wine vinegar

8 cups (1.9 L) beef stock

2 (.07-oz [2-g]) packages Italian dressing seasoning

Preheat the oven to 325°F (163°C).

Place the heads of garlic in an aluminum foil pouch, add the olive oil and salt and roast the garlic in the oven for 30 minutes. I place the little foil pouch on a pan in case there's any leakage during the roasting process. These garlic heads can be done in a larger quantity if you wish. I usually buy a few pounds of garlic at a time and keep them in a sealed container in the fridge for up to 2 weeks. It's so nice having heads of garlic that you can just squeeze into whatever you like. The best way to do that is to just barely remove the top of the head with a sharp knife and squeeze from the root to the tip.

Season the chuck roast or short ribs with the salt and pepper, and, in a large Dutch oven, sear the meat in olive oil until it is golden brown on both sides. Remove the seared meat from the Dutch oven for a few moments.

On the stovetop over medium heat, add the onions, carrots, celery and mushrooms to the Dutch oven and sweat them for 10 minutes. Next, deglaze the Dutch oven with the tomatoes, wine and red wine vinegar, removing all the golden goodness from the bottom of the pan. A wooden spoon works great for this.

Add the meat back to the Dutch oven, letting it rest on top of the bed of sweating veggies.

Create a braising liquid by combining the beef stock with the Italian dressing seasoning, stirring well to avoid lumps of seasoning. Add the braising liquid to the Dutch oven. The meat should be covered completely with liquid. This ensures that it will not dry out.

Bake the roast in the oven for a few hours. The meat will let you know it's done once it's fork-tender.

I like to serve my roast in a bowl with fresh celery leaves and a few cloves of roasted garlic. This dish makes great leftovers and is easy to reheat for several days. I'd venture to say it would also freeze well, but there's never any extra Sunday roast lying around for that.

LIVER AND ONIONS AND CELERY ROOT MASH
with BACON GRAVY

I like to use veal liver because it has a far more delicate texture and flavor than an adult cow's liver does. I recommend purchasing the liver from a butcher shop as they will slice it for you. It's important to ask a lot of questions and pay attention as to what artisan butchers are doing behind the counter to fulfill all your culinary fantasies.

SERVES 4

½ lb (228 g) bacon

2 white sweet onions, cut into ¼-inch (6-mm) slices

4 tbsp (60 ml) Worcestershire sauce

¼ cup (38 g) cornstarch

½ cup (125 g) all-purpose flour

1 tsp garlic powder

1 tbsp (15 g) sea salt

1 tsp freshly cracked black pepper

1½ lb (683 g) veal liver cut into ¼- to ½-inch (6- to 13-mm) thick slices lengthwise (remove the skin and pat the liver dry with a paper towel before seasoning)

2 tbsp (28 g) butter

3 cups (720 ml) cold water or stock

¼ cup (60 ml) apple cider vinegar

CELERY ROOT MASH

2 to 3 lb (910 g to 1.5 kg) celery root

1 tbsp (15 g) salt

2 tbsp (28 g) butter or a few more (my pants from last summer don't fit, so how much butter you want to add is up to you)

5 cloves chopped garlic

1 tsp red chili flakes, optional

8 oz (228 g) sour cream

1 to 2 cups (240 to 480 ml) celery root simmering liquid (depending on the thickness you're looking for)

Salt and freshly cracked black pepper, to taste

Preheat the oven to 350°F (177°C). Cut the bacon into ¼-inch (6-mm) cubes or, if you're using platter-style bacon, just cut it into strips. Sometimes if I don't want to contaminate my cutting board with raw bacon, I'll use a pair of kitchen shears and cut the bacon right over the pan I'll be cooking it in. Add the bacon, onions and Worcestershire sauce to an oven-safe pan (such as a cast iron pan).

Bake the bacon uncovered for 15 minutes or until golden brown. I like to use a wooden spoon to stir the bacon every so often. As the bacon renders, it acts as the fat to caramelize the onions. That's what I call killing two birds with one stone. The smell of bacon and onions is also intoxicating. It's my version of aromatherapy. Why aren't there candles that smell like this?

While the bacon and onions are marrying each other in the oven, combine the cornstarch, flour, garlic powder, sea salt and pepper. I tend to toss all the dry ingredients together in a large bowl and I'll give 'em a nice whisk with a fork.

With a potato peeler, remove the exterior skin of the celery root. Think of it as a really large, fragrant potato. That being said, remove any weird spots or notches. Cut the celery root into large chunks and toss them into a large pot of salted boiling water so that they are completely covered.

In about 15 minutes, the celery root will be soft and tender and ready to mash. Strain off the hot cooking liquid into the sink while you catch the celery root in a colander. Reserve 1 to 2 cups (240 to 480 ml) of the liquid for the mash.

While the celery root is drying off for a few moments, place the now-empty pan back onto the stovetop. On medium heat, sauté the butter, garlic and red chili flakes until the garlic is slightly golden brown. Then add the cooked celery root to the pot. I like my mashed veggies a little chunky. You can easily obtain the texture by mashing them by hand in the pot with a fork. Finish the mash with the sour cream, simmering liquid and salt and pepper. After the mash is made, cover it with a lid on low heat to keep warm.

Carefully remove the hot bacon and onions from the oven and start cooking them on the stovetop over medium heat. Coat veal livers with the cornstarch mixture. Make a large well in the middle of the pan to sear the veal liver in and add the butter. Sear for about 4 minutes on one side and then 3 on the other. Remove slices from the pan and set them aside on a plate.

Now it's time to make the bacon gravy. The residual cornstarch from the veal liver acts as the thickening agent for this old-school treat. With a wooden spoon, I start to slowly incorporate the bacon and onions with the pan drippings left from the seared liver. In the culinary world, the delicious, brown flavor drippings left in pans is known as fond. It makes sense to me that it is named this, because I am very fond of its flavor. The best way to remove this epic flavor is typically with an acid, such as vinegar or bourbon. In this case, feel free to use either, but my grandma uses the water and apple cider vinegar with her wooden spoon.

Bring this gravy to a low simmer while stirring frequently. After about 5 minutes of solid simmering, the gravy will take shape. I finish my gravy with freshly cracked black pepper and salt. Add the liver back to the gravy and enjoy over the celery root mash. This dish makes awesome leftovers.

DRUNKEN SHANKS *with* ROOT PUREE

I love the flavor of this sauce. It's so very earthy and pure. Red wine really is worth the buy, as it makes this dish sing. The flavor from the root veggies permeates the meat throughout the slow-and-low cooking process. Root veggies are available year-round. Once you purée them all together, they take on a completely different flavor profile. You'll love it.

SERVES 4

4 (2-inch [5-cm]) beef shanks (also sold as meaty soup bones) or beef shanks steaks

1 cup (150 g) carrots, large dice

1 cup (150 g) white onion, large dice

1 parsnip, cut into 4 pieces

1 sweet potato, cut into 1-inch (2.5-cm) rounds

2 sprigs fresh rosemary, leaves removed and roughly chopped

2 cups (480 ml) red wine

4 cups (960 ml) homemade beef stock (page 117) or store-bought beef stock

I love to effortlessly prepare this in a slow cooker. There's little to clean up and it's easy to put away. Place the soup bones or shanks, carrots, onion, parsnip, sweet potato and rosemary in the slow cooker. Cover with the red wine and beef stock, then cover the slow cooker with the lid and you're good to go.

Let your slow cooker roll at medium-low heat for at least 3 hours or until the beef is fork-tender. Once done cooking, remove the beef from the slow cooker.

Use an immersion blender to purée the cooked root vegetables. It's up to you how thick you want the sauce to be. I like mine silky smooth. Serve hot. Makes great leftovers in the fridge for up to a week.

Butcher Babe Tips

* If you don't have an immersion blender, you can use a fork to mash up the tender root veggies. I call this outcome "rustic" and there's nothing wrong with that!

* Different root veggies to try include radish, yucca, celery root (also known as celeriac), parsnip, daikon and beet.

BARBECUE BRISKET AND COLLARDS
with PEACH BARBECUE SAUCE

Peaches are what happens when the earth decides to make its own candy. A peach should be sweet and sour all at the same time. That's why it seems only natural to make a tangy barbecue sauce out of them! What could be more savory than using peaches that have been cooked down in the buttery fat of a beef brisket?

SERVES 6

2 tbsp (14 g) smoked paprika

1 tbsp (15 g) freshly cracked black pepper

3 tbsp (42 g) packed brown sugar

4 to 5 lb (1.8 to 2.3 kg) corned brisket

4 tbsp (60 ml) vegetable oil

4 cups (960 ml) pickle juice

5 cloves garlic

1 tsp red chili flakes

4 cups (960 ml) cold water

1 bunch collards (about 2 lb [910 g] or more; they cook down to nothing like spinach does)

PEACH BARBECUE SAUCE

1 lb (455 g) fresh or frozen peaches, cleaned, cut into large pieces (if you're using fresh, remove the skin and pit; I don't recommend using canned peaches)

3 tbsp (21 g) smoked paprika

1 tbsp (15 g) salt

2 tbsp (28 g) packed brown sugar

In a pie tin, mix together the smoked paprika, pepper and brown sugar to create the dry rub for the brisket. I like to use pie tins because they are easy to clean and cheap to purchase. Also, they keep you from putting raw meat on your cutting surfaces.

I like to score the top of my brisket on the fat side in a crosshatch pattern. The best way to do this is with a very sharp knife. Basically, you're just cutting little squares on the meat, being careful not to cut into the flesh hiding under the fat cap. The dry rub adds a lot of flavor once it's tucked away deep inside those little nooks and crannies.

In a hot, oiled Dutch oven, sear the brisket fat-side down until golden brown, which takes about 5 minutes. Flip the brisket over so that the fat side is up and add the pickle juice, garlic, red chili flakes and water.

Rip the collards into large pieces and tuck them around the brisket, burying them in the liquid. Turn the oven on to 325°F (163°C). The brisket should be barely covered with liquid.

It might seem strange, but I like to toss my peaches in the smoked paprika, salt and brown sugar and gently set them in a little pile on top of the brisket. I will then put the entire dish in the oven for 3 hours at 325°F (163°C). I don't cook this with the lid on because I want the peaches to caramelize as the brisket cooks.

Once the dish is done, I will remove the peaches with a pair of tongs and set them aside in a small sauce pan to continue to cook down just a bit further. I find that about 15 minutes on medium heat works great. I like to serve the peach barbecue sauce in a rustic chunky style right on top of the slices of brisket.

I leave the collards in the pan. The brisket will be placed on a cutting board to slice. Serve hot.

(continued)

Butcher Babe Tips

* Feel free to use a number of different greens in this recipe, such as kale and rainbow chard.

* Do you know how to pick out the perfect peach? Depending on what time of year it is, the best peaches may not be available to you. Here's what I do—I let my nose do the work. If it doesn't smell like a peach, how can it taste like one? The same can be said for just about any other fruit or vegetable. Step two in the peach interviewing process: I let my hands do the work. The more ripe, or soft the peach is, the more developed its flavor will be. I don't mind using very ripe peaches for things like cobblers or barbecue sauces. If I'm slicing them up for a salad or a snack, then I'm going to need the texture of a less ripe peach. On the opposite side of the spectrum, you don't want to crack open a rock hard peach. The perfect peach should be fragrant, free of any puncture wounds and have a slightly soft flesh.

EAST-MEETS-SOUTH SHORT RIBS
with FIG GLAZE AND CILANTRO PESTO

Short ribs are awesome. They are easily one of the most flavorful pieces of meat on the cow. Even though they are a little bit pricey, I still jump at the chance to purchase and cook them. If you can't find any, don't fret because chuck roast works as a great substitute. They come from the same neighborhood on the cow, anyway. The chuck is like the neighbor of ribs. If you want to skip the following braising procedure, then have the short ribs cut "Korean style." They will be cut into ¼-inch (6-mm) pieces versus huge chunks. You will still want to cover them in the dry rub, but you can go straight to the grill instead of the Dutch oven. If you choose this quicker method, just give them a brush of fig glaze after you hit the grill and you're almost ready for dinnertime.

SERVES 6

2 tbsp (30 g) salt

1 tbsp (7 g) Chinese five-spice powder

1 tbsp (15 g) freshly cracked black pepper

5 lb (2.3 kg) short ribs or chuck roast (if you use chuck roast, cut it into 6 equal chunks)

2 tbsp (30 ml) vegetable oil

3 cups (720 ml) cold water

FIG GLAZE

½ lb (228 g) dried figs

3 oz (85 g) fresh ginger, peeled (a plastic spoon works great to peel fresh ginger)

2 oz (57 ml) bourbon

CILANTRO PESTO

¼ lb (114 g) roasted cashews

1 bunch fresh cilantro (stems are fine)

Zest of 2 limes

Juice of 2 limes

2 tbsp (30 ml) rice wine vinegar

1 tsp salt

1 tsp red chili flakes

Mix together the salt, Chinese five-spice powder and pepper and apply the dry rub liberally to the surface of the short ribs. In a large Dutch oven over medium-high heat, sear off the beef in vegetable oil. This takes some time and care. Make sure you get every side seared off so that the meat is golden brown.

Preheat the oven to 325°F (163°C). Cover the beef in enough cold water to submerge them and roast them in the oven for about 2½ hours, or until tender. If you are using short ribs, it's a good sign that they are done once you can easily remove a bone from them.

To make the fig glaze, add the figs, ginger and bourbon to a food processor and pulse until smooth. Remove the glaze from the processor and store in an airtight container. This will last for several days under refrigeration. I like to brush the meat with the glaze and place it right onto the grill just until a little bit of color has developed. This doesn't take long.

Pulse the cashews, cilantro, lime zest, lime juice, rice wine vinegar, salt and red chili flakes in a food processor until smooth. Pour the Cilantro Pesto over cooked short ribs. This pesto lasts for 2 days in the fridge. If I know I'm not going to be able to use it before it goes bad, I will freeze it in an ice cube tray. I do that with a lot of things, and I totally recommend it.

Finish the short ribs with the fig glaze and cilantro pesto and call it a day!

LUNCH BOX ROAST BEEF *with* HORSERADISH CREAM

I worked at the butcher shop for years, and I loved a lot of things about it. One of the things I hated, though, was slicing processed lunch meat for its patrons. So many people would ask for the low-sodium stuff. I would often find myself trying to encourage them to make their own lunch meat if they were really so concerned about the nutritional content of it. This recipe can be the first milestone for you if you too are a lunch meat junkie.

SERVES 6

¼ cup (23 g) finely ground coffee

3 tbsp (45 g) kosher salt

3 tbsp (45 g) freshly cracked black pepper

2 tbsp (6 g) fresh thyme leaves

3 lb (1.4 kg) eye of the round

4 tbsp (60 ml) Worcestershire sauce

HORSERADISH CREAM

4 oz (113 g) freshly prepared horseradish or fresh horseradish, peeled and grated

8 oz (228 g) sour cream

1 tbsp (15 g) salt

1 tsp freshly cracked black pepper

Preheat the oven to 375°F (191°C).

Grind the coffee, salt, pepper and thyme in a food processor until smooth to create a dry rub. Cover the eye of the round completely with the dry rub and Worcestershire sauce and place it in a shallow baking dish. Roast the meat in the oven for 35 minutes or until an internal temperature of 135°F (57°C) has been reached. This will give you a nice rare look after it's been sliced. You can cook it longer if you'd like, depending on how rare you like the beef. I let mine cool quickly by placing it in the freezer for about an hour. This makes the cooking process stop as well as making it much easier to slice. With a very sharp knife, I'll slice it as thin as I can.

This is great practice for learning how to carve meat also. I'll place the nice chilled slices in an airtight container. Once the entire piece is sliced, I will douse it in the Worcestershire sauce. This meat stays nice and fresh for up to 3 days under refrigeration. You can also roast up several pieces of round this way and freeze them whole to then be sliced weeks later. Just make sure you wrap it up well so that it won't get freezer burnt.

To make the horseradish cream, mix together the horseradish, sour cream, salt and pepper in a small bowl and store refrigerated for up to 2 weeks. Serve on top of the Lunch Box Roast Beef. Yum.

Before cutting the roast, let it rest and chill in the freezer. Firmly hold the roast in one hand and slice with the other. Here, I'm removing the "face" of the roast and about to make it my snack.

I try to cut the roast as thinly as I can, in one smooth and fluid motion. You don't want to saw the meat. I hope you have a sharp knife.

THYME-CRUSTED RIBEYE ROAST
with APRICOT MUSTARD

Ever since I was a little girl, ribeye has been my favorite cut of meat. It's so flavorful and juicy and laced with ribbons of buttery fat. It's one of the most forgiving cuts of meat for this reason, and luckily it's nearly impossible to overcook and dry out.

Fresh thyme and beef pair together like sugar in my sweet tea. The only way that this dish of amazing proportion could get any better is with a lil sweet and sour note. I know some of you steak sauce fans are like "What will I do without my steak sauce?!" Do what the French did and put some apricot-infused stone ground mustard on your steak. Its tart and earthy fruit notes will leave you slightly embarrassed you were having steak sauce cravings in the first place.

SERVES 6-10

5 tbsp (75 g) kosher salt

5 tbsp (75 g) freshly cracked black pepper

1 bunch fresh thyme, leaves only

5 to 8 lb (2.3 to 3.6 kg) boneless ribeye roast

Butcher's twine

APRICOT MUSTARD

8 oz (228 g) dried apricots

4 oz (113 ml) bourbon or brandy

8 oz (228 ml) large-grain mustard

Preheat the oven to 500°F (260°C).

Combine the salt, pepper and thyme for the dry rub. Set aside. Tie the roast with the butcher's twine, sectioning off the portions you will want for your guests. For example, a 5-pound (2.3-kg) roast that is tied 8 times with butcher's twine can account for up to 10 guests who will receive about an 8-ounce (228-g) portion of ribeye. Trussing and tying this roast also helps keep it in a uniform shape to ensure the best result and yield.

Roast the meat in the oven in a shallow roasting tray on a grate. This slight separation of the protein from the pan allows for more hot airflow so the meat cooks much quicker. I start all my larger roasts out on high heat at 500°F (260°C) for the first 15 minutes and then finish it slow-and-low at 325°F (163°C) for the remainder of the cooking process. I like to serve my roast beef at a nice medium-rare, so I cook it to an internal temperature of 135°F (57°C) and pull it out of the oven. The phenomenon known as carry-over cooking still continues to raise the internal temperature once the meat has been removed from the oven. You can always bring meat up to a higher temp, but you can't go backward.

In a small saucepan, bring the apricots and bourbon to a simmer. This cooks out the boozy flavor of the bourbon and also softens up the apricots, making them easier to purée. In a food processor, mix the apricot mixture and mustard together until smooth. This sauce is best served at room temperature. Refrigerate it up to 2 weeks.

Butcher Babe Tips

* There are several different grades of beef in the United States. The best is called USDA-Prime. It has the highest amount of marbling, or fat, resulting in a buttery taste and texture. There is no dish in real life called "prime rib" but there is a ribeye that may be graded as prime.

* The second is USDA-Choice. Choice has a lower amount of marbling. I often recommend that a choice ribeye roast is purchased over prime. Ribeye is already such a "fatty" cut, not to mention that price of choice versus prime is very different. It can be half the price at times.

* The third grade I'd like to mention is USDA-Select. The grade has even less marbling. Fat equals flavor remember. This is a nice grade to use for making jerky (see page 118).

WHOLE BEEF TENDERLOIN
with GREEN AND PINK PEPPERCORN RUB

A whole beef tenderloin, also known as a WBT in the butchery world, on average weighs about 4 to 5 pounds (1.8 to 2.3 kg) after the chain, silver skin and fat have been removed. I've trimmed and tied about one thousand of these things for clients' holiday gatherings over the years. It's really not that difficult as long as you've got a sharp knife, a meat thermometer and some butcher's twine.

I've come up with a foolproof method on how to get the perfect holiday roast every time. This recipe screams, "Happy Holidays!" instead of, "What the heck am I gonna make for dinner?"

SERVES 8-10

4 to 5 lb (1.8 to 2.3 kg) WBT

3 tbsp (75 g) green peppercorns

3 tbsp (75 g) pink peppercorns

3 tbsp (45 g) kosher salt

2 tbsp (30 ml) olive oil

Butcher Babe Tip

A substitute for butcher's twine is unwaxed dental floss, dye- and flavor-free (unless you're going for that minty flavor).

You can clean the WBT yourself at home by removing the chain and working around the fat that separates the muscle from the inedible silver skin, or you can go to a butcher shop and have them do that for you. Most shops will also truss and tie the whole loin for you as well. The fun part about trussing and tying the meat yourself is that you get to see how many portions you will have for your guests. The most stressful thing I've witnessed in the butcher shop was buyers' fear that there wouldn't be enough meat. Generally speaking, a WBT at 5 pounds (2.3 kg) will feed 10 people with an 8-ounce (228-g) portion per person. An 8-ounce (228-g) portion is pretty hearty, if you ask me. Let's get to cooking this thing.

About 1½ hours before your guests arrive, preheat your oven to 425°F (218°C). Truss and tie the meat, tucking the tapered tail end on the tenderloin under itself so that you've got a streamlined shape for the oven to roast.

In a small bowl, combine the green peppercorns, pink peppercorns and salt to create a dry rub. Cover the tenderloin in the olive oil, then the dry rub, set it on a roast pan and put it in the oven. It's time to relax because in 15 minutes you'll turn your oven down to 325°F (163°C) and it'll be smooth sailing for the next 30 minutes.

Because every oven if different, you'll want to start checking the internal temperature of the tenderloin at this point. I like a nice 135°F (57°C) for mid-rare. After you remove the tenderloin from the oven, let it rest for 15 minutes and you're good to go.

FILET *with* BOURBON BLUE CHEESE SAUCE

Oh, there's nothing quite like a filet; the beautiful tender chunk from the tenderloin. The filet is revered for its tender-like qualities. I've witnessed it being enjoyed from rare to well-done. (I don't recommend well-done.) From a classical perspective, blue cheese and beef go together like peas in a pod. I made a similar version of this sauce in Vegas when I was on the tenth season of *Food Network Star*, when Giada De Laurentiis, who isn't even a fan of blue cheese, thought it was delicious. What can I say—I put bourbon in it.

SERVES 2

2 (8-oz [228-g]) filets

1 tbsp (15 g) kosher salt

1 tbsp (15 g) freshly cracked black pepper

1 tbsp (15 ml) vegetable oil

2 tbsp (28 g) butter

1 large tomato, fine dice

1 scallion, cut on the bias

¼ red onion, small dice

BOURBON BLUE CHEESE SAUCE

4 cloves garlic, crushed

2 tbsp (28 g) butter

4 oz (113 ml) bourbon

1 tsp red chili flakes

1 tsp salt

1 cup (240 ml) heavy whipping cream

5 oz (113 g) smoked blue cheese (regular blue cheese is fine too)

Preheat the oven to 450°F (232°C).

Season the filets with salt and pepper.

In a screaming-hot cast iron pan add a touch of vegetable oil, sear the filets 5 minutes on one side then flip them over. Add a nice little fleck of butter on each filet, then finish roasting at 425°F (218°C) for 6 more minutes. Pull the filets out of the oven and remove them from the hot pan. Let them rest for 10 minutes for the perfect mid-rare.

To make the bourbon blue cheese sauce, sweat the garlic, butter, bourbon, red chili flakes and salt in a small saucepan. Once the sauce has reduced by half, remove it from the heat and add the cream and blue cheese. Mix together with a large spoon until incorporated and it starts to thicken up. Right before you serve the sauce, make sure to toss in the tomato, scallion and red onion.

Basting the filet in butter after removing it from the oven. I may or may not have a butter problem.

There are a ton of different types of blue cheese. Some are more subtle than others. Here are some examples of less abrasive blues (from basic to briney): Bayblue, Dolcelatte, Saint Agur and Gorgonzola.

HOOSIER RIBEYE *with* VIDALIA ONION CHUTNEY

I grew up in a family of farmers. I love to garden, play in the dirt and hit up a few state fairs during the summer. One of the most iconic bites from a Midwestern fair is a Hoosier ribeye. In the state of Indiana, we have more than just sprawling fields of corn. A real Indiana Hoosier knows how to make a killer ribeye. I love this fair bite because it cooks up fast on the grill, is easy to eat on the go and the Vidalia onion chutney has a summery kick, like a glass of sweet tea.

SERVES 2

1 tsp salt

1 tbsp (15 g) freshly cracked black pepper

1 tsp packed brown sugar

1 tsp smoked paprika

2 (5- to 6-oz [142- to 170-g]) thinly cut ribeyes

1 tbsp (15 ml) vegetable oil

VIDALIA ONION CHUTNEY

1 tbsp (14 g) butter

1 large Vidalia onion, cut into strips or julienned

¼ cup (60 ml) bourbon

¼ cup (60 ml) red wine vinegar

2 tbsp (28 g) packed brown sugar

1 tbsp (15 ml) Dijon mustard

1 tsp freshly cracked black pepper

To make the dry rub, combine the salt, pepper, brown sugar and smoked paprika. Cover both sides of the steaks thoroughly with the dry rub. Place both steaks on a hot and seasoned grill or pan. The pan should sizzle when the steaks start cooking. These cook up so quickly, taking only about 3 minutes per side. I like to use a cast iron pan, because I cook the Vidalia onion chutney in the steak drippings. If you'd rather grill them, just make the onions in a saucepan.

On high heat, add the butter to the pan and toss in the onion. It should start to sear the second it hits the pan. I like to let the onion sit there for 5 minutes and brown. Next, add the bourbon, and don't catch anything on fire. (I set off fire alarms a lot.)

Let the bourbon cook out and then add the red wine vinegar. Reduce the sauce and the heat again. It's important to stir this frequently so it won't burn.

To finish the onion chutney, add the brown sugar, Dijon mustard and pepper. You can use this Vidalia onion chutney for a number of things other than this steak. It stays fresh for weeks in the fridge. Serve the chutney right on top of the steak. I love to plate mine up with a few tomato steaks covered in salt and pepper. This combo is great on a toasted bun if you're on the go.

Invest in only the best dried herbs and spices, stored in airtight containers.

Aluminum pie dishes work great for dry rub stations and protect your other work surfaces from raw meat contamination.

Adding the bourbon straight from its bottle into a hot pan can be dangerous. It's much safer to pour from a small dish. I pour it from the bottle though, because I'm a trained professional. Be careful, y'all.

Once again, you caught me with the butter. It's like meat lip gloss: don't leave home without it.

PORTERHOUSE *with* PAN SAUCE

I can't think of anyone who doesn't like a "two for one" type of deal. Buying a porterhouse is kind of like that. Basically you're getting a strip steak and a filet all in one go. The flavors are straight up classical French, as thyme and beef go together like me in some red lipstick. The combination can never go wrong, considering I'm about to show you how to prepare an obnoxiously big steak, and then have a garlic-infused pan sauce from its drippings. Dang!

SERVES 2-4

1 (2-inch [5-cm]) thick porterhouse steak (trim any excess fat; you can season your pan with it)

3 tbsp (45 g) kosher salt

1 bunch fresh thyme, leaves only

2 tbsp (17 g) whole black peppercorns

2 feet (60 cm) butcher's twine

3 cloves garlic

2 oz (57 ml) bourbon

3 oz (85 g) butter

A porterhouse is like the great-grandpa of a T-bone. What I mean is that a porterhouse has a larger section of filet. To be exact, the filet's width must bigger than 1 inch (2.5 cm) to be considered a porterhouse. I personally don't think that a little dinky inch section of filet hanging on a T-bone screams porterhouse to me. I like to go big. I mean really big. So when I cut an obnoxiously big porterhouse, I cut it 2 inches (5 cm) thick, from the sirloin end of the cow. The plus is that the filet will be huge; the minus is that there will be a ribbon of unchewable bubblegum-like tissue in a portion of the strip steak as it runs into the sirloin in the hind quarter. I'm showing off here anyway, so I'll just cut my losses while I cook up a 2½-pound (1.1-kg) piece of meat.

I have a coffee grinder in my house just for dry rubs. The best way to make this classical French-inspired rub is in one of these. Using the coffee grinder, combine the salt, thyme and peppercorns. The dry rub is done when it all is one texture, and you will find that the color is a nice forest green.

I tie my porterhouse horizontally on the cutting board so that the filet is nice and snug against the rest of the huge steak. I wouldn't want the filet to overcook; that would be a travesty.

Cover the steak with the dry rub. Season an oven-safe pan, such as a cast iron pan, with any fat trimmings you had or 1 tablespoon (15 ml) vegetable oil and heat it over medium-high heat. Once there is a nice coating of fat in the pan and you can barely see a haze of heat rising from the oil, it's time to set down your steak. Start your porterhouse, as with any other bone-in thick cut of meat, so that it's standing up on its bone. Yes, the steak should be pointed up, facing the sky. This is a necessary step with any thick-cut, bone-in meat. If you do not follow this step, the steak will be undercooked and raw (in some cases, closest to the bone). The bone adds a ton of flavor but also can act as an insulator to the protein you are so lovingly preparing.

You should hear a searing sound immediately. Let the big ol' steak get a nice crust. This takes under 10 minutes. Preheat your oven to 400°F (204°C). I invite you to use your nose in the kitchen and start to keep a catalog of what different levels of browning smell like. We all know what burnt smells like. The trick is browning food to nearly burnt, but not burnt so that we can enjoy the caramelized flavors that the Maillard reaction produces. Essentially, we are caramelizing the carbohydrates in foods.

(continued)

Trim any excess fat. Ideally about ¼ inch (6 mm) of fat is sufficient for me. I store fat trimmings in the freezer to season my cast iron pan with.

Your thyme salt rub should be ground until it's a smooth powder, similar to flour. If you use a coffee grinder, clean it out with soap and water before brewing your next cup o' joe.

I like to ensure this steak cooks evenly so I truss it with butcher's twine. I'm pulling the filet portion of the porterhouse inward towards the bone so it won't overcook.

Pat the steak thoroughly with the dry rub, getting every little nook and cranny.

Carefully set the porterhouse bone-side down in the pan. It should stand up on its own, but if it doesn't, give it a hand.

Lovingly set the garlic on the steak. Is there any other way to do it?

PORTERHOUSE *with* PAN SAUCE *(continued)*

Take a peek at the seared bottom of the steak before laying it down in the pan to sear on one side. Brown for 5 minutes before giving it the flip of approval and continuing to cook it in a 400°F (204°C) oven for 15 to 20 minutes. Add the cloves of garlic at this time and allow them to caramelize in the hot pan. I like to cook my porterhouse to an internal temperature of 135°F (57°C). Once the steak has hit your desired internal temperature, remove the pan from the oven and pour in the bourbon, letting it bathe the garlic in its luscious flavor. Remove the meat from the pan and let it rest for 15 minutes. Add the butter to the pan also; reserve this sauce for the steak once it's rested and has been cut.

A classical way to serve this meat monster is to remove the strip and the filet individually from the bone. Slice and fan the steaks where they used to be intact right next to the iconic T-bone. Pour the sauce over the steak and get ready to call it a night—after you take some pics, of course.

SOUTHERN-FRIED STEAK *with* PECAN BUTTER

I can't really think of anyone who doesn't like a piece of meat covered in flour and fried in a cast iron skillet. Well I can think of a few people, but they happen to be vegan. This old Southern classic goes great as a main dish, covered in gravy or on a sandwich. You can also use round steak, pork loin or even a chicken cutlet. Anyway, it's gonna be delicious.

SERVES 4

PECAN BUTTER

1 tbsp (15 ml) bourbon, optional (molasses or brown sugar works great too)

½ tsp freshly cracked black pepper

3 oz (85 g) pecans (small pieces are fine)

4 oz (113 g) butter, softened

Zest of 1 lemon

1 tbsp (3 g) parsley

SOUTHERN-FRIED STEAK

4 (5-oz [142-g]) cutlets of meat

1 tbsp (15 g) salt

1 tbsp (15 g) freshly cracked black pepper

¼ cup (38 g) cornstarch

2 cups (480 ml) milk

2 whole eggs

1 sleeve saltine crackers, crushed to powder

½ cup (62 g) flour

½ cup (76 g) cornstarch

1 tbsp (15 g) salt

1 tsp freshly cracked black pepper

2 cups (480 ml) vegetable oil

In a saucepan, bring the bourbon, pepper and pecans to a boil and reduce the liquid by half. Set aside to cool. Fold the chilled bourbon mixture into the softened butter along with the lemon zest and parsley.

On a piece of plastic wrap or parchment paper, lay out the compound butter in a 4-inch (10-cm) tube shape. Fold one side of the parchment paper or plastic wrap on the butter's right side. Take the remaining plastic or parchment that's facing you and pull it over the mixture so that it becomes taut and a cylinder starts to form. Lastly, fold the remaining side over to enclose the pecan butter. Once this is formed and sealed so it's airtight, I like to keep it stored in the freezer. It lasts for weeks that way and is so easy to slice once it's frozen.

I set up 3 individual breading stations in 3 separate pie dishes, and use a pair of chopsticks to effortlessly move the meat from one pie dish to the next.

Season both sides of the cutlets with the salt and pepper, then sprinkle them with the cornstarch. Make sure to shake off any excess cornstarch.

In the first pie dish, mix the milk and eggs with a whisk until well incorporated. In the second pie dish, mix together the crushed saltine crackers, flour, cornstarch, salt and pepper. Dip the seasoned cutlets into the milk mixture. Then, dip the soaked steaks into the saltine cracker mixture and set them aside.

In a large cast iron pan, bring the oil to medium heat. I use a little test my grandma taught me when frying: once you think your oil is at the appropriate temperature for frying, sprinkle in a few little specks of flour; the little specks should immediately start to fry and turn golden within moments, they should not start to burn. Or you can use a thermometer to get the oil around 350°F (177°C).

Once you get your oil temperature all figured out, gently place the coated steaks in the oil and start to fry them. Always lay down anything you're going to fry away from you as a safety measure. You never want to just throw anything into a pan carelessly. These steaks take about 5 minutes on each side, or until the level of brownness you're looking for is achieved. They should be at least 150°F (66°C) on the inside.

When removing the steaks from the oil, place them on a dish covered in a few layers of paper towels. This will give them a chance to cool down and the paper towels will soak up any extra oil.

I often salt and pepper my steaks again once they are done cooking, but that's just me. Right before I serve them, I will top them with a nice piece of pecan butter and off they go.

These steaks are best served fresh and hot shortly after they have been made. If you wish to reheat them a day later, baking them in the oven at 350°F (177°C) for 15 minutes will bring them back to life.

BEEF TONGUE TACOS

Imagine the most flavorful, silky chuck roast you've ever had. The luscious layers of beef that just fall apart in your mouth, leaving an unforgettably buttery finish and leaving you wanting more. Well, quite honestly, that's what beef tongue will do for you if you cook it right. I'm going to show you a quick and easy way to utilize a not-so-popular cut of meat. I know what you're thinking: "EWW."
Why don't you try something new because quite honestly, beef tongue is hands down one of my favorite cuts of meat.
Trust me. You already bought the book! HA!

SERVES 6

1 large white onion, rough chop

4 cloves garlic, whole

2 tbsp (29 g) butter

2 tbsp (30 g) salt

1 tbsp (6 g) ground black pepper

4 bay leaves, whole

1 tbsp (8 g) smoked paprika

2 lb (907 g) beef tongue, fresh not frozen

4 quarts (4 L) cold water

1 pack fresh corn tortillas

1 bunch cilantro, washed and rough chopped with stems, for garnish

1 bunch radishes, washed and greens removed, for garnish

2 fresh limes, cut into wedges, for squeezing on top of the taco

In a large saucepan or Dutch oven on medium-high heat, sauté the onion and garlic with the butter until slightly brown. At this time add the salt, pepper, bay leaves and smoked paprika.

Heating up the dried spices in the pan actually "wakes them up." Lay the whole pieces of beef tongue in the pan and add the cold water. Turn the heat on to medium-low, just so the pot's contents are barely simmering. Place a lid on the pot and let it cook "slow-and-low" for about 3 hours or until fork-tender. Once the beef tongue is nice and tender, remove it from the liquid and let it rest on a cutting board for about 15 minutes or until it's cool enough to handle.

Remove the butter lining of the tongue by peeling it off with a paring knife or spoon and discard. Cut the tongue into 1-inch (25-mm) cubes. Save the braising liquid from the beef tongue and use it as a stock in any recipe. It does great in the freezer too.

Bring a medium-size saucepan to high heat and add a few tablespoons of the braising liquid to sear the tongue in. Gently add the cubes of tongue to the pan and sear them on high heat for about 5 minutes. Turn them over to brown more than one side with tongs or a fork. Once they are nice and crispy set them aside and start to build your taco!

Place two corn tortillas in the pan that you just cooked the beef tongue in. Lower the heat down to medium heat. Add a few splashes of the braising liquid to the pan before each addition of a tortilla, unless you have a pretty large saucepan. If not, just do one batch of two tortillas at a time. Cook the corn tortillas for about 2 to 3 minutes on each side then set aside on a clean dish for serving. Place a few chunks of tongue on each and garnish with cilantro, radish and a squeeze of lime. Enjoy!

PIMENTO BURGER

I've got to admit there is nothing like a burger. It does not matter where you're at in the world, there will be some version making you feel like you're at home. While there are countless meat combinations, toppings and breads, the following recipe is the version I have fallen in love with. This sandwich is like a chunk of meat on a salad, surrounded by two large, cheese smeared croutons, also known as buns.

MAKES 4 (8-OZ [228-G]) BURGERS

1 lb (455 g) brisket

1 lb (455 g) chuck

2 tbsp (30 ml) vegetable oil (for the grill)

1 tbsp (15 g) kosher salt

1 tbsp (15 g) freshly cracked black pepper

¼ cup (60 ml) Worcestershire (for basting)

1 head iceberg lettuce or any other crisp greens

Salt and freshly cracked black pepper, to taste

1 red onion

1 tomato

Burger buns

PIMENTO CHEESE

2 cups (222 g) Havarti cheese, shredded (or any type of melting cheese)

3 cloves garlic, crushed

1 tbsp (15 ml) hot sauce, such as Louisiana brand

1 (4-oz [113-g]) jar diced pimentos, drained

1 jalapeño, diced (if you're feeling spicy; I know I am)

½ cup (110 g) mayo

Salt and freshly cracked black pepper, to taste

REFRIGERATOR PICKLES

1 bunch radishes

1 cucumber

1 stalk celery

1 bunch fresh dill

3 scallions

3 cups (720 ml) red wine vinegar

2 cups (480 ml) cold sweet tea (or water plus 3 tbsp [42 g] packed brown sugar)

1 lemon, sliced into 4 slivers

Peeled garlic cloves

(continued)

Grind the brisket and chuck at home or buy it from a butcher shop. If you can't get either brisket or chuck, just go with an 80/20 burger mix (it's the fattiest). Fat = flavor. Enough said.

I grind my brisket and chuck once and patty them into shape. After the burgers are formed, rub them with oil and season them with the salt and pepper, then set them aside. Prepare the grill or a pan for these bad boys with the vegetable oil. Make sure it's nice and hot and that just a touch of oil has been introduced. More often than not, burgers get torn up because the cooking surface wasn't hot enough, the grill wasn't seasoned or clean, and they weren't ready to be flipped yet. A good way to tell if a protein isn't ready to be flipped is if it's sticking to the pan. Just leave it alone! Don't play with your meat.

The shape of my burgers depends on the size of bread they will be served upon. There's nothing more annoying than having to search for your burger patty under a ton of bread or making a mess because you're basically eating a hunk of meat in between 2 crackers. One time I screamed, "Where's the beef?" at a barbecue and everyone just stared at me. The bread for your burgers is as important as the burger mix itself. It must be toasted. I repeat: it must be toasted. I like to toast my buns covered in pimento cheese as my burgers rest.

To make the pimento cheese, mix together the cheese, garlic, hot sauce, pimentos, jalapeño, mayo and salt and pepper in a medium bowl and set aside. This cheese mixture will be the spread you put on the buns for your burger! You can set the buns, covered in a ½-inch (13-mm) layer of this addicting cheese, on the upper rack of your grill or in the oven on a sheet tray for 10 minutes on 350°F (177°C) or until golden brown.

OK, now it's time to dress the burger. Everyone is different, of course, but this is how I like to get down:

Rip off a piece of lettuce from the head of iceberg equivalent to the size of the burger you're having. Add some salt and pepper and you're good to go. The iceberg lettuce in particular is wonderful at keeping tabs on any sauces you like on your burger. So if you're a mustard or ketchup fan, now's the time to stake your claim. (Store iceberg lettuce for several days in the fridge, wrapped in moistened paper towels. Under those brown wilted layers, there's bound to be some crisp pieces.)

I love onions. Like, a lot. I don't care if my breath stinks later, I just ate the best burger I've ever had. I cut my red onion for burgers horizontally from the root so that I have beautiful rings of onions. The thickness depends on your cut of onions.

The problem with tomatoes is that there really are only a few months of the year where they make fireworks go off in my mouth. Notably, the summer months produce the fragrant heirloom varieties that make my winter tomato cravings drive me wild. When a tomato is good, it's euphoric. From the outside in, it should smell like a tomato. The fruit itself should be firm with a slight spring when held. The texture should be silky and buttery, not mealy and gritty. Many great tomatoes are ruined when put under refrigeration. I never keep mine in there—they will just turn to mush. As far as seasoning them, a little salt and pepper and you're good to go. I have a thing for tomatoes, actually. Sometimes I meet people who don't like them but I just remind them that they haven't met the right one. If I can't find the perfect tomato, I'd rather go without.

Speaking of certain veggies only being available during certain times of the year, now is the perfect time to bring up pickles. Pickles allow you to keep things fresh for seasons to come. A quick and easy method is a Southern tradition we refer to as "refrigerator pickles." It does not include the labor-intensive process of canning anything under heat. Essentially, you just clean veggies, cut them into desired shapes, put them into a clean glass jar and pour a pickling liquid over them. Keep the jar's contents sealed with a lid and let them ride for weeks in the fridge.

To make the pickles, fill a mason jar about three-fourths full with the radishes, cucumber and celery. Stuff the dill and scallions around the vegetables. Top off the veggies and herbs in the jar with the red wine vinegar, sweet tea or water, lemon slivers and garlic cloves. Give the jar a good shake and you're done. I find myself doing this a lot when I'm cleaning out my veggie drawers, and I encourage you to do the same. The combinations and flavor profiles of pickles are endless.

MEAT LOAF *with* TOMATO JAM

It took me a while to admit it publicly, but I love meat loaf. I was embarrassed for several years by the fact that I loved to sneak slices of it cold, right out of the pan in the fridge with a piece of fluffy white bread. I would use the piece of bread as a serving utensil and grab what would fit in my hand. I got so good at it that I could also get a nice amount of sauce too. I'm sure my grandma knew what I was doing late at night when I was enforcing the No Meat Loaf Left Behind Act I am so passionate about. Maybe meat loaf helps me sleep? Meat loaf = food coma? Probably.

SERVES 10

2 white onions, small dice

1 (2-oz [57-g]) package French onion soup mix

3 tbsp (42 g) packed brown sugar

¼ cup (60 g) salt

3 tbsp (45 g) freshly cracked black pepper

1 stick (4 oz [113 g]) butter

4 cups (960 ml) beef broth

2 cups (161 g) instant oatmeal

5 lb (2.3 kg) 80/20 ground beef

6 whole eggs

TOMATO JAM

5 lb (2.3 kg) ripe tomatoes, roughly chopped

2 whole white or red onions, small dice

2 cups (440 g) packed light brown sugar

2 cups (480 ml) apple cider vinegar

4 oz (113 g) smoked paprika

¼ cup (60 ml) mustard

¼ cup (60 g) salt

2 tbsp (30 g) freshly cracked black pepper

Preheat the oven to 350°F (177°C). On the stovetop, sauté the onions, French onion soup mix, brown sugar, salt, pepper and butter together over medium heat until the onions become translucent. Then add the beef broth to the pan along with the oatmeal. Stir frequently until the oatmeal is done cooking.

In a large bowl, mix the sautéed onion mixture with the ground beef and eggs until combined. Transfer the meat loaf mixture to a large casserole dish, smoothing out the meat loaf mixture so that is it evenly distributed in the pan, leaving about 1 inch (2.5 cm) or so from the top of the dish for the tomato jam. If necessary, use 2 casserole dishes to cook the meat loaf. You can get fancy if you like and form it into various shapes. You could even bake it in a Bundt pan. Seriously.

As far as I can tell, everyone's got an idea of what a good barbecue sauce tastes like. I'm all about using tomatoes out of the garden before they go bad and making a ton of tangy tomato jam. It goes on everything as far as I'm concerned, especially this meat loaf.

In a large pot over medium heat, combine the tomatoes, onions, brown sugar, apple cider vinegar, smoked paprika, mustard, salt and pepper and slowly simmer. Let the mixture reduce by nearly half, stirring frequently so that it does not burn. Pour the jam over the meat loaf and bake the loaf, covered with foil, for 30 to 45 minutes. If you have any extra jam left over, it freezes wonderfully and makes a great condiment for just about anything, especially chili in the winter when delicious tomatoes can't be found.

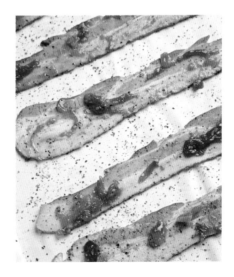

STEAK TARTARE *in* AVOCADO BOWLS

If I could eat only one thing for the rest of my life, this would be it. It's healthy and fresh and filling. Everything about this dish just rubs me the right way. The avocado is silky and buttery, just like the raw meat. If you haven't had Steak Tartare, there's a first time for everything.

SERVES 2

1 egg yolk

Dash hot sauce

1 tsp Dijon mustard

¼ tsp freshly squeezed lemon juice

¼ tsp Worcestershire sauce

Salt and freshly cracked black pepper, to taste

1 tbsp (13 g) small dice shallot

¼ tsp red chili flakes

1 tbsp (3 g) fine dice fresh parsley

1 tsp small dice jalapeño, seeds removed

1 (5-oz [142-g]) filet or sirloin (beef or lamb work very well)

1 ripe avocado, cut in half and pit removed

Fresh lemon zest, for garnish

To make the tartare base, whisk together the egg yolk, hot sauce, Dijon mustard, lemon juice, Worcestershire sauce and salt and pepper in a small bowl until combined. Toss in the shallot, red chili flakes, parsley, jalapeño and salt and pepper and, last but not least, cut the meat by hand right before you are going to eat it. I cut mine into very small ¼-inch (6-mm) pieces. I take mine from the fridge to the cutting board to the mixing bowl. Serve the tartare immediately after dividing it in half between the 2 avocado pieces and garnish with lemon zest. You can eat this with a fork as is or with crackers, crostini or chips. Enjoy immediately. Steak Tartare is not safe to save as leftovers.

Chapter 2

THE LAND OF BACON AND OTHER PINK DELICACIES:
~ Pork ~

Bacon. I said it. Now I've got your attention. Did you know that bacon is really just smoked pork belly? That's right, bacon doesn't just appear out of nowhere, people. A whole slab of bacon can weight up to 20 pounds (9 kg). Pork is easily the most versatile protein consumed and the list of meat-derived products from this nearly 700-pound (318-kg) adult animal is longer than you might expect. We use the intestines for casing when making sausages. We use its skin for pork rinds. We smoke its belly for bacon. We make pets out of them and train them to find rare mushrooms, such as truffles, in various parts of the world.

Pork is so dang good because of its buttery taste and texture. Some more obscure, heritage varieties of pig have a sweeter flavor that I very much prefer. I'm not a fan of mass-produced pork. It doesn't taste quite right to me and it doesn't feel right ethically. Most smaller, locally owned butcher shops will carry local breeds of pork. Breeds with names like Berkshire, Duroc and Red Wattle, among others. My favorite breed is the mangalica. They have coarse, curly hair all over their cute bodies. Once you invest in these more heritage breeds of pork, I'm positive you will taste the difference.

SIXTY-MINUTE CARNITAS

When I hear the words "cilantro," "beer" and "lime," I get hungry. Even if I wasn't hungry before, I can't help myself. If you take these South-of-the-border fixin's and add some spicy chipotles and pork, 60 minutes later it'll be dinner time. It's a misconception that cooking pork butt has to take several hours. I cut the cooking time in thirds by using pork butt steaks that are thinly cut versus one big piece that weighs up to 10 pounds (4.6 kg) whole. You can use this method for various other types of meat also.

SERVES 4

1 tbsp (7 g) ground cumin

1 tbsp (15 g) salt

1 tbsp (7 g) red chili flakes

1 tbsp (14 g) packed brown sugar

1 tbsp (7 g) chili powder

3 tbsp (45 ml) vegetable oil

2 (1-inch [2.5-cm] thick) bone-in pork butt steaks

16 oz (480 ml) beer or cold water

2 cups (480 ml) cold water

1 (3-oz [85-g]) can diced or whole chipotle peppers

Juice of 2 limes

1 bunch fresh cilantro, stems and leaves chopped

1 red onion, small dice

Mix the cumin, salt, red chili flakes, brown sugar, ground chili pepper and vegetable oil together in a medium bowl and coat the pork steaks with it. In a large cast iron pan, sear both sides of the pork steaks over medium-high heat until both sides are golden brown. Turn down the heat to medium and add the beer, cold water, chipotle peppers, lime juice, cilantro and onion. Using the empty chipotle-pepper can, keep adding cold water until the steaks are submerged. (Using the empty can rinses it out and transfers that lovely chipotle flavor from the can to the braising liquid.)

Simmer the steaks, covered, for 45 minutes over low heat so that the protein can break down. If you let the liquid boil rapidly, it will cause the meat to become tough. Slow-and-low is the ticket here.

Remove the pork steaks once they are tender and shred them on a cutting board. Now it's time for tacos, enchiladas, salads and whatever else you are hungry for!

Butcher Babe Tips

* You can reduce the braising liquid and turn it into a sauce for your carnitas.

* The pork butt isn't actually a butt at all. Did you know it's actually the shoulder of the animal? The bone in the pork butt is actually part of its shoulder blade. Another term for this cut of meat is "Boston butt."

SMOKY ROOT BEER BUTT
and ROOT BEER BARBECUE SAUCE

I like to make things easy. Life is too short to not know some practical tricks that can be applied every so often.
The following recipe is a kitchen hack I love implementing. You get the flavor of a smoky grill without all the mess of the smoker.
Root beer acts as a sweet and tangy braising liquid that can be easily transformed into a quick barbecue sauce.
The acidity of the root beer also helps to tenderize the pork.

SERVES 12

1 (8-lb [3.6-kg]) pork butt, cut into 3 pieces (I prefer bone-in pork butt)

½ cup (121 g) kosher salt

1 cup (220 g) packed brown sugar

1 cup (237 ml) Dijon mustard

1 cup (237 ml) molasses

1 tbsp (7 g) cayenne pepper

2 tbsp (14 g) cumin

4 tbsp (28 g) smoked paprika

1 tsp cinnamon

3 tbsp (21 g) cocoa powder

2 liters root beer (I love Barq's Root Beer; orange soda is good also)

ROOT BEER BARBECUE SAUCE

2 cups (440 g) packed light brown sugar

2 cups (480 ml) apple cider vinegar

1 (4-oz [113-g]) can tomato paste

Salt and freshly cracked black pepper, to taste

1 cup (237 ml) yellow mustard

1 cup (237 ml) Worcestershire sauce

½ cup (76 g) cornstarch

1 cup (240 ml) cold water

Preheat the oven to 400°F (204°C).

I like to tie each piece of pork butt around the circumference of the meat with butcher's twine because it helps when handling it down the road. Make the dry rub mixture by combining the salt, brown sugar, Dijon mustard, molasses, cayenne pepper, cumin, smoked paprika, cinnamon and cocoa powder in a medium bowl. Rub the dry rub generously over each cut of meat and roast them on a sheet tray for 15 minutes. This little visit to the oven will wake up all those lovely oils in the dried spices while also creating a crusty little flavor profile on the outside of the pork.

Remove the pork from the oven and transfer the pork butt to a slow cooker. If you do not have a slow cooker, then use a large Dutch oven.

Pour the root beer over the pork until completely covered and cook for 2 to 3 hours on medium heat. You can easily pick up a portion of pork during the cooking process by using a fork to grab it by its twine. When the pork is done cooking, it will fall off the bone and/or shred effortlessly. Remember to remove the twine before serving or putting up for leftovers.

In a medium saucepan over medium heat, combine the brown sugar, apple cider vinegar, tomato paste, salt and pepper, yellow mustard and Worcestershire sauce. Cook until the sauce is simmering.

In a medium measuring cup, combine the cornstarch and cold water, whisking well to remove lumps. When making a slurry, you must always use a cold liquid to activate the cornstarch and thicken sauces. Add the slurry to the simmering sauce, and continue whisking until sauce comes to a boil, about 8 minutes.

Great. It's almost dinnertime. Fire up the grill and dip the pork butt in the sauce then place it directly on the grill's grates over open flames. Let the fire flavor and sear the cooked pork. After about 15 minutes on the grill, remove the meat and place it in a large pan (I like to use disposable aluminum pans) and shred the pork. Make shredding easy and use 2 forks while it's still warm. Cover the pork in the Root Beer Barbecue Sauce and call it a day. This dish is great to cook up ahead of time. You just simply reheat the pork with sauce and serve at a party away from home. Cheers.

Store the root beer barbecue sauce in the refrigerator. The sauce will stay fresh stored in the refrigerator for up to 2 weeks.

PEACHES AND CHEEKS *and* BROWN BUTTER CORN

Peaches are a universal symbol of the South. I think they are the cutest of all the fruits. For goodness' sake, they are even covered in fur! They come in a variety of colors inside and out and they smell like heaven. When you're looking for the perfect peach around the month of August, it should smell like one. The ripest flesh should be slightly soft to the touch, like a ripe avocado. If the peaches aren't ripe yet, you can speed up the process by storing them in a brown paper bag or you can slow the ripening process by keeping them in the fridge for a couple weeks.

This delicious dish is best served at room temperature—if you can wait that long to dig in!

SERVES 4

2 lb (910 g) pork cheeks or pork belly

Salt and freshly cracked black pepper, to taste

2 tbsp (30 ml) vegetable oil

1 white onion, small dice

1 cup (180 g) celery, small dice

1 large tomato, roughly chopped (seeds and skin are fine)

3 dried bay leaves

2 cups (480 ml) apple juice (or 2 cups [480 ml] apple cider vinegar mixed with ¼ cup [55 g] packed brown sugar)

8 cups (1.9 L) homemade chicken stock (page 117) or store-bought

1 bunch fresh thyme, tarragon or parsley

6 fresh, ripe peaches, peeled, pitted and sliced into 6 pieces each

BROWN BUTTER CORN

12 fresh ears corn, in the husk

1 (4-oz [113-g]) stick butter

6 cloves garlic, slivered

¼ cup (60 ml) bourbon or apple cider vinegar

1 tbsp (15 g) salt

1 tbsp (15 g) freshly cracked black pepper

2 tbsp (28 g) packed brown sugar

Preheat the oven to 300°F (150°C). Season the pork cheeks with the salt and pepper. Heat the vegetable oil in a large pan over medium-high heat and sear the pork cheeks on both sides. Remove the pork cheeks from the pan and set aside. Reduce the heat to medium. Add the onion, celery, tomato and bay leaves to the pan and sweat them in the pork fat. Yum.

Return the pork cheeks to the pan and roast the cheeks in the oven, uncovered, for 2 to 3 hours or until fork-tender in the apple juice and chicken stock. Remove the cheeks and bay leaves from the sauce and continue to reduce until nape. "Nape" means until it's thick enough to coat the back of a spoon. Add the cheeks back to the sauce before you serve them. Now's a great time to taste the sauce once it's reduced. Lots of people make the mistake of heavily seasoning a dish with lots of salt before it's reduced, resulting in a very salty sauce. So if it still needs salt, now's the time to do it.

Moments before you serve the dish, sprinkle the cheeks with the leaves from the bunch of fresh thyme. This herb makes the dish sing. If you don't care for thyme, however, tarragon is another substitute. If you can't get either thyme or tarragon, fresh parsley will do in a pinch.

If you can't get fresh peaches, then buy 1 pound (455 g) of frozen ones from the store. Let them thaw, laid out on a plate in the fridge and covered with plastic. About a half hour before you serve this soulful dish, pull them out of the cold so they can come to room temperature. You'll never see me touch a can of store-bought peaches, even if my life depended on it.

Cut off the bottoms of the corn cobs, exposing the kernels on the opposite end from the pesky corn hairs. That way, you can remove them easily after grilling.

Soak the whole ears of corn in lukewarm water for 20 minutes in the kitchen sink. While the corn is soaking, preheat a grill to 350°F (177°C). Shake any excess water off the corn and place the ears of corn on the grill. They should make a slight searing sound; if they don't the grill is not hot enough. Rotate them every so often. They will cook in about 30 minutes. Remove the ears of corn from the grill and let them come to room temperature.

(continued)

Remove the husks from the corn by simply pulling them away from the cob. How easy is that! Now for another tip. It's always tricky to get the kernels off the corn cob. Grab a small stainless steel bowl and flip it over. Place that upside-down bowl into a large bowl. Use the little indentation on the upside-down bowl as a nest for the base of your corn cob. With a serrated knife, remove the corn from the cob. The larger bowl will catch all the corn as you remove it from the cobs. This little trick has saved me so much time over the years. I also like to save my corn cobs for stock down the road. If I don't happen to have a use for them immediately, I will just put them in the freezer in a plastic bag.

In a large pan, brown the butter for the corn. This is really easy to do if you have a sense of smell. Place the butter into the pan along with the garlic. Making brown butter with garlic in it helps you keep track of how far along your butter is being cooked.

Once the garlic has reached a nice, light golden brown, your butter should be what is considered brown butter. You will notice some white fluffy bubbles appear as the butter cooks. Those are just fat solids congealing, or burning off. These fatty solids are the culprit of the undesired burnt taste that can develop while cooking with unclarified butter. Anyway! They are just fine where they are with this dish as long as you don't burn your garlic butter.

Brown butter can easily get away from you. This is not the type of thing that you start to make and then ignore. Within a matter of moments, it's done. Take the pan off the heat as soon as the butter has browned and pour in the bourbon. Add the salt, pepper and brown sugar and set aside. You will use this wonderful concoction when you reheat your corn moments before you serve it with the Peaches and Cheeks. Don't worry, your guests can't get a buzz from the corn. The bourbon will cook off when you sauté it.

Place the hot pork cheeks and sauce on top of the corn. Last but not least, place a few slices of fresh peaches on top and call it a day! I've heard this makes great leftovers, but I've never seen any.

COUNTRY RIBS *with* SWEET TEA SAUCE

OK, so, what exactly is a country rib? Well, realistically, it is just a bone-in pork chop that's been split down the middle, leaving a nice long section of meat to effortlessly enjoy with two little bones to nibble at on either end. They are pretty inexpensive and can easily be made to feed a lot of people.

It's easy to see how many you'll need for your guests because you can count on the average person eating one and a big eater having two. There is also little fat to be found on these guys, so you must be careful not to overcook them. They are easy to grill and even easier to roast in the oven. They don't fall apart like baby back ribs or pork butt, but they easily have just as much flavor with far more meat for your buck. This cut of meat is one of my favorite from the pig, as it's easy to eat and goes great with a glass of iced tea. Or in this case, a sauce made from it.

SERVES 4

4 lb (1.8 kg) country ribs

2 tbsp (30 g) salt

1 cup (240 ml) molasses or sorghum (blueberry sorghum [page 69] is awesome)

Wood chips

6 oz (170 g) black tea

SWEET TEA SAUCE

6 small bags black tea

3 cups (720 ml) hot water

3 cups (660 g) packed brown sugar

1 cup (240 ml) apple cider vinegar

Zest of 8 lemons

Juice of 8 lemons

Place the country ribs in a large bowl. In a small bowl, combine the salt and molasses. Pour the molasses mixture over the ribs and rub it on the meat until the ribs are completely covered in the molasses mixture. Allow any excess to drip off before transferring the ribs to the smoker.

Soak your wood chips of choice and mix in the black tea. Preheat your smoker to 220°F (104°C). This method starts off at a higher heat, accounting for the fact that you lose quite a bit of heat when you open the smoker.

Place the country ribs in the smoker and cook for 1 hour or less. Ideally, you want to maintain a temperature of 170°F (77°C). Begin checking the meat for doneness after 35 minutes of cooking time, using a meat thermometer to check for an internal temperature of at least 160°F (71°C). Remove the country ribs from the smoker and set aside.

To make the sweet tea sauce, steep the bags of black tea in the hot water for 20 minutes and remove the tea bags, squeezing any excess moisture out before discarding them. Add the brown sugar and apple cider vinegar and stir frequently until it reaches a thick syrup. After it's become a very thick, candy-like consistency, add the lemon zest and lemon juice as it reaches room temperature. This sauce will knock your socks off. It lasts for weeks in the fridge. If you need to bring it back to its candy-like state, I suggest adding 1 cup (240 ml) water into a pan with the sauce and slowly bringing it up to medium heat while stirring frequently. Bourbon works too.

Dip the country ribs in the sweet tea sauce. Serve immediately.

SWINE APPLE

I remember the first time I saw a pineapple growing in the wild. I was surprised by the fact that it grew close to the ground in a strange spikey bush in the middle of nowhere on Maui. I was farming for a month on the Hana side of the island and I fell in love with the island and the flavors that originated there. This showstopping dish embodies those feelings all over again every time I make it. This recipe takes a little bit of love. It's worth every drop of sweat though, I promise. Mahalo!

SERVES 4

1 ripe pineapple, top removed and reserved, sides peeled with a serrated knife

½ lb (228 g) boudin or 1 country rib, bones removed, for the filling (if the rib doesn't fit as is, just cut it down a bit)

1½ lb (683 g) sliced bacon (about 21 slices of bacon cut platter-style)

Butcher's twine, cut into at least 12 (1-foot [30-cm]) long pieces.

2 tbsp (11 g) whole cloves

Preheat your oven to 350°F (177°C).

After cleaning and carefully removing the skin and core of the pineapple, fill with the boudin and it's time to wrap it in the bacon. There's a ton of ways to do this, actually. I feel like the least stressful way is the best way. Even if it ends up looking less than perfect, let's be real here, people—it's a pineapple covered in bacon; it can't taste bad!

Bacon cut platter-style is neither thick nor thin; rather, it's what most people consider just right. On a slicer at a butcher shop, it's about ⅛-inch (3-mm) thick.

On a large surface, lay out 2 feet (60 cm) of plastic wrap. Horizontally, lay out the butcher's twine about 1 inch (2.5 cm) apart from the one above it so that it is the size of your pineapple. Lay more butcher's twine now vertically, starting in the very middle of your twine checker board. It's very important to keep the butcher's twine straight for the sake of the Swine Apple's presentation.

Start to lay out the bacon slices, one barely overlapping the other, over the pieces of twine. Try to place the pieces of bacon so that the twine is right in the center of each piece. It took me a few tries to get the hang of this myself. It's OK if it's not perfect.

Once your bacon is all set and ready to become one with the stuffed pineapple, place the fruit on its side in the very center of the mix. I use the plastic wrap to pull the bacon around the pineapple so that I can start to tie the twine and secure it. It's butcher shop knowledge to also work from the center out when tying in most all cases. Don't fret about the excess string for now—you can cut it later.

After I have secured the horizontal pieces of twine, I'll wrap a nice and tight string around the "equator" of the pineapple. Lastly, I start from the very center with tying the vertical ones and the worst part is almost behind you. Very gently, turn the Swine Apple over from its downward-facing side. The face of this portion is known as the presentation side and is the portion you will present to your guests.

Now for the whole cloves. Place them in the center of the butcher's twine hash marks. They taste delicious and are reminiscent of the little dimples of the whole pineapple. Use the long, skinny parts of the whole cloves to pierce the skin of the bacon so that it is secured. Throw away the plastic wrap.

Place the raw Swine Apple in a high heat–safe dish and place it in the oven, presentation-side up. Let it roast for about 40 minutes or until its internal temperature reads 160°F (71°C). If it's browning too quickly in your oven, cover it with foil throughout the cooking process to protect it.

Let the Swine Apple rest on its side in the pan for up to 10 minutes and transfer it to a serving dish. Secure the top of the pineapple to the fruit with a wooden skewer and watch your creation disappear.

TENDERLOIN STUFFED
with SWEET POTATOES AND GOAT CHEESE

I love this dish because with a little butcher's twine, you can transform something everyday into a pretty elevated surprise.
I often find myself using the starchy sides from the meal before and reinventing them inside cuts of meat like this all the time.
All you need is a sharp knife, confidence and some leftovers.

SERVES 4

1 large pork tenderloin, not trimmed (usually between 1½ and 2 lb [683 and 910 g])

1 tsp salt

1 tsp freshly cracked black pepper

2 tbsp (30 ml) Dijon mustard

2 feet (60 cm) butcher's twine

1 tbsp (3 g) fresh thyme

1 orange, sliced in half and zested

FILLING

1 cooked sweet potato, peeled or unpeeled

1 tbsp (15 ml) honey

2 oz (57 ml) melted butter

4 oz (113 g) goat cheese (preferably cranberry or herb-infused goat cheese)

Preheat the oven to 350°F (177°C).

Place the tenderloin on a cutting board. From the top-facing portion of the tenderloin, cut a straight 1-inch (2.5-cm) deep crevasse about 5 to 6 inches (13 to 15 cm) long from its head to its tail. Season all the surface area of the meat with the salt, pepper and Dijon mustard.

For the filling, mix together the sweet potato, honey and melted butter in a medium bowl until the desired smoothness is reached. Crumble in the goat cheese so that it stays intact.

Fill the tenderloin with the filling mixture. Loosely tie the tenderloin about 4 times with twine just to keep the tenderloin intact. Cover the tenderloin with the fresh thyme, sliced orange and orange zest. Roast the tenderloin in the oven for about 25 minutes. Squeeze the roasted-orange juice over the tenderloin. Let the meat rest for 5 minutes. Serve hot.

Starting from the center of the tenderloin, place your first tie. You will learn from trial and error when the trussing is too tight or too loose. Experience is the best teacher.

Brush the tenderloin with any remaining Dijon mustard.

CHAI PINEAPPLE JAM *for* HOLIDAY HAM

I should have started a holiday food emergency help line a few years ago. You wouldn't believe all the things I've heard on the phone speaking to thousands of frantic meat buyers. I had to realize eventually that not all things that have to do with food are common sense for home cooks. Once I realized that simple fact, my phone conversations became a lot easier. The quicker they could articulate what they wanted to see on the kitchen table, the faster I could help them get there. More often than not, they didn't even know what it was they wanted, so I told them. You want this ham whether you know it or not. You're welcome.

Do you know how to order a ham? What's the difference between the butt end and the shank end? Well, let's start with the flavor profiles. Just because it's a ham does not mean it's been smoked. A fresh ham is just that—it hasn't been chemically processed in any way, shape or form. A smoked ham actually is smoked, and they are available whole or spiral-sliced, bone-in or boneless. Seems pretty straightforward, right? Let's continue.

I recommend 1 pound (455 g) of ham per person, generally speaking. That's 16 ounces (455 g) of delicious meat sure to get you full at least once at the dinner table and then again to supply guests with a small amount of take-home treasure.

I prefer to let the guys in the smoking industry smoke my hams. Nueske's brand makes my favorite holiday ham. They have a ton of varieties and flavor profiles. These hams have already been cooked. Essentially, you are reheating them. The best way to do that is in the oven, covered with foil. The foil tent ensures that the ham won't dry out.

I'm a big fan of buying the butt end, spiral-sliced hams and making my own sauce so I can hide it inside the ham's nooks and crannies as it reheats to an internal temperature of at least 151°F (66°C).

MAKES 1 QUART (947 ML)

6 bags chai tea

4 cups (960 ml) apple cider

1 whole cleaned and cored pineapple, cut into small pieces

1 tsp ground cloves

1 cup (240 ml) bourbon

2 cups (440 g) packed brown sugar

This jam can be made days in advance of when you'll need it. In a medium saucepan over medium-high heat, steep the bags of chai tea in the apple cider until it reduces by half. Remove and discard the tea bags. Add the pineapple, cloves, bourbon and brown sugar and keep cooking the mixture until it comes to a rolling boil. It will start to thicken up significantly at this point. Store the Chai Pineapple Jam sealed in a glass jar under refrigeration for weeks. Makes a great gift.

APPLE-BRINED CROWN ROAST
with BOURBON BROWN BUTTER

There is something so regal about a crown roast. It's as beautifully hearty as it is classical. The look of awe on your guests' faces when it makes it to the table makes every dang bone worth Frenching after all. The roast looks expensive as can be, but it's not that pricey at all. For just a few dollars a pound, you can be the new owner of about 15 pounds (6.8 kg) of meat and a crown roast. One cool thing about creating it at home is that you get to keep all the trimmings for sausage! I had about 5 pounds (2.3 kg) of pure profit when I was done. It's good to keep a bowl to collect your scraps for sausage.

I had the butcher shop remove the chime bone from the back of the loin so I wouldn't have to remove it at home with my handsaw. I specifically order two rib halves of the pork loin, not the one near the pork shoulder. You will have about ten ribs on both whole loins.

Remove the membranes from the back of the ribs. With the bones facing downward, remove the flap of skin that's facing upward. Once you start to remove it, a natural seam will be seen and you can run your knife along it until it's removed. Once you start to fabricate more meat at home, you will begin to notice that the meat will let you know where to go.

Even though the local butcher kindly removed the chime bones from the loin, I still had to remove some feather bones from the underside of the loin with a paring knife. If you are more comfortable using a knife, I recommend using a boning knife instead. Continue to feel around the loin with your hands and cut out any extra bones that may get in the way.

Now it's time to French the bones. Take about 1½ inches (4 cm) off the meat from the tip of the ribs toward the loin. To French the bones, begin by cutting downward toward the loin at a 45-degree angle on the insides of the rib bones. I like to come back after I've removed the meat and, in a downward motion, scrape the bones clean.

SERVES 10

8 cups (1.9 L) apple cider

1½ cups (362 g) sea salt

2 cups (440 g) packed brown sugar

Juice of 2 oranges

4 tbsp (28 g) TANG orange drink mix powder

15 lb (6.8 kg) crown roast pork loin

2 tbsp (30 g) salt

1 tbsp (15 g) freshly cracked black pepper

1 tbsp (14 g) packed brown sugar

1 bunch fresh thyme, leaves only

1 tbsp (7 g) smoked paprika

BOURBON BROWN BUTTER

1 cup (240 ml) bourbon

1 stick butter

Zest of 1 orange

1 tbsp (3 g) fresh thyme leaves

In a large plastic tub, make the apple brine by mixing together the apple cider, salt, brown sugar, orange juice and TANG until the salt and brown sugar have dissolved. Lay both sides of the Frenched pork loins down in the liquid. Both loins should be nearly submerged. Cover the tub with plastic wrap. Brine the pork for at least 6 hours and up to 12 hours.

Remove the pork loins from the brine and pat dry. On a clean surface, lay both loins down so that they are together with the ribs facing down. I bought the largest sewing needle (reminiscent of a butcher's roast needle) I could find and gently bent the end of it so I could sew through the meat more easily.

(continued)

APPLE-BRINED CROWN ROAST
with BOURBON BROWN BUTTER *(continued)*

Preheat the oven to 350°F (177°C).

With a 2-foot (60-cm) piece of butcher's twine, I carefully joined the 2 loins. You don't want to pull the twine too tightly or you will rip the meat. There's a fine line here, but I have faith you'll find it. Now that I am joining the 2 loins together and creating the iconic crown shape, I will start behind one rib and sew it through to the other loin behind an opposite rib. If you have someone around to help you hold this while you sew, now's a great time to ask for help.

Sew the roast together from top to bottom, making about 6 incisions from one point to the next so that, ideally, they appear seamless. This roast can be prepared in advance and held under refrigeration for up to 48 hours. I don't recommend cooking it hours ahead of time as it is difficult to reheat, and you will run the risk of drying it out.

Create the dry rub by mixing together the salt, pepper, brown sugar, thyme and smoked paprika in a small bowl. Cover the roast with the dry rub. Protect the bones from the cooking process by wrapping them in aluminum foil. Place the roast in a large cast iron skillet. I stick a raw apple in the middle of my roast to help hold the roast's shape while cooking.

Cook the roast until an internal temperature of 155°F (68°C) is reached. This takes about 1 hour. Remove the roast from the oven and let the roast rest for 15 minutes. Remove it from the cast iron skillet and set it on a serving dish, with the apple intact. Portion the chops between the Frenched bones after removing the foil. Remove the butcher's twine before serving.

To make the bourbon brown butter, heat the roasting pan over medium-high heat on the stovetop and pour in the bourbon and cook until it starts to reduce. Bourbon is a great ingredient for removing the yummy brown dripping from the pork bones. Add the butter and let it melt for about 10 minutes. Cook until a nice and nutty flavor starts to develop. Pull the pan from the heat and add the orange zest and thyme. The sauce is ready to go. Go ahead and take a seat—you deserve it.

(continued)

Chime bone is removed and set atop the pork loin. Any good butcher shop would be happy to do this for you, as removing the bone by hand requires a meat saw and is pretty dangerous.

Showing a visual example of how the chime bone is removed. From top to bottom, chime bone (or a portion of the back bone) atop the bone-in pork loin.

What the eyes may miss, the hand will see. It's important to feel around the loin and remove any remaining chime bone.

Begin removing the membrane from the far end of the loin by using a paring knife.

Continue to remove the membrane. If it's hard to grasp, use a paper towel.

Peel back the ribs from the loin (by applying light pressure in a downward motion) no more than 4 inches (10 cm) from the loin.

With your fingers, remove the fat cap membrane from the pork loin and save it for grinds.

Once you start to remove the fat cap membrane, use a sharp knife to completely remove it, if need be.

Depending on what size the roast is, you might need to trim excess meat from the roast so it can form a nice and circular roast.

Make an incision on the center of each rib bone from the base closest to the crown roast to the tip of the rib.

You will make this cut on the underside of the rib, then one incision horizontally at the base of the cut, almost like a letter "T." Be sure to make the incision all the way to the tip of the rib bone. This will aid in peeling away the excess, resulting in a Frenched bone.

An experienced meat cutter or chef would use a boning knife, but a paring knife will work just fine. Lay your knife at a 45-degree angle and get to scraping!

I find it the easiest to scrape all the meat off the bones by starting at the "T"-shaped incision, away from myself. It's also safer this way.

Remove any other excess meat between the ribs. This might take a while.

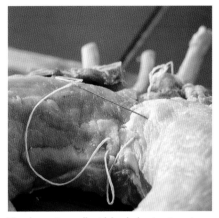

Thread a trussing needle with butcher's twine. A trussing needle is a hearty version of a sewing needle with a bent tip.

Place the pork roasts next to each other so that both loins meet. With the Frenched bones laying directly on the cutting board, start to sew the loins together. Allow at least ½ inch (13 mm) of roast on both sides.

Gently pull the twine through the roast, continuing the procedure until the roast appears to be one. Repeat the process on the opposite side, and secure the sides by making a knot.

In order to guarantee uniformity, I like to tie another piece of twine around the entire roast.

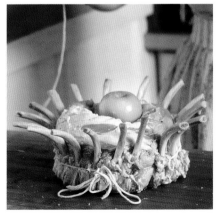

Place an apple in the center to help the crown roast keep its shape while cooking.

Place foil tightly on each rib bone so that they won't burn during the cooking process.

HAM STEAK *with* SWEET POTATO TATER TOTS AND BLUEBERRY SORGHUM

Have you ever had a ham steak? My grandma always used to sear them up in her cast iron for me. A half-inch thick (13 mm) and delicious, this smoky treat is sure to please any bacon lover. A smoked ham steak is already cooked, so reheating it is quick and easy. Not to mention the Sweet Potato Tater Tots and a tangy blueberry sauce. Yes, that's a thing. Hold on to your belt buckles.

SERVES 2

TATER TOTS

2 sweet potatoes

1 tsp cinnamon

2 tbsp (30 ml) honey

1 egg

3 cups (177 g) breadcrumbs, such as panko, divided

1 tsp salt

BLUEBERRY SORGHUM

½ cup (50 g) fresh blueberries (blackberries are great too)

1 tbsp (15 ml) freshly squeezed lemon juice

½ cup (120 ml) sorghum

1 tbsp (14 g) butter

2 (½-inch [13-mm]-thick) ham steaks

Preheat the oven to 400°F (204°C). Bake the sweet potatoes whole, wrapped in foil, for about 40 minutes or until fork-tender. Remove them from the oven and scrape the fluffy insides into a bowl, discarding the skin.

Add the cinnamon, honey, egg, 1 cup (60 g) of breadcrumbs and salt to the sweet potatoes and mix until the potatoes are smooth. (I use a fork and that works just fine.) Now it's time to form the tots. Lay out the sweet potato mixture in a cylindrical shape on a large piece of plastic wrap or parchment paper. Fold over the plastic wrap so that you can form that classic shape. Fold over the ends of the plastic wrap and let the sweet potato mixture chill in the freezer for 1 hour, or until it is stiff enough to cut into 1-inch (2.5-cm) pieces.

Right before frying the tater tots, roll them in the remaining 2 cups (118 g) of breadcrumbs. Once they are ready to go, gently place a few at a time in a 325°F (163°C) vegetable oil bath on your stovetop. When they are done, they will float to the top of the pan. Skim them out carefully and sprinkle them with some salt.

In a small saucepan, cook down the blueberries and lemon juice over medium heat. I like to muddle the berries with a fork as they intensify in flavor. This only takes about 5 minutes. Add the sorghum. This wonderful stuff packs a punch in the flavor department.

Melt the butter in a medium sauté pan over medium-high heat. Add the ham steaks and cook for 10 minutes or until the steaks are golden brown and crispy.

Serve the blueberry sorghum warm on top of a smoky ham steak with the sweet potato tater tots. If you wanted to fry up a few eggs, this might be the most perfect breakfast dish ever.

BONE-IN LOIN CHOPS *with* SOURDOUGH SAGE STUFFING

When I was growing up, I was never thought of as a skinny kid. Thanks, Grandma! Grandma Susie cooked everything with a bone in it in a cast iron skillet. I love this about her. She really knew how to get flavors out of dishes she created. This one-pan wonder gets me every time. It's hot and crispy and super filling. Plus, it's pretty inexpensive and easy to make.

SERVES 4

4 (¾-inch [19-mm]-thick) bone-in loin chops

1 tsp salt

1 tsp freshly cracked black pepper

STUFFING

4 raw eggs

4 cups (960 ml) stock (beef, veggie, fowl or pork—see page 117)

1 tbsp (3 g) finely chopped fresh sage

1 tbsp (15 g) salt

1 tsp freshly cracked black pepper

1 white onion, small dice

4 stalks celery, small dice

2 large carrots, small dice

5 to 6 cups (296 to 355 g) 1-inch (2.5-cm) cubed sourdough bread (old bread is perfectly fine)

Season the pork chops with salt and pepper and set aside. They will bake on top of the stuffing as it crisps up in the oven.

Preheat the oven to 350°F (177°C) and place a medium cast iron skillet inside to heat up.

In a large bowl, mix the eggs and stock together with a whisk. Add the sage, salt and pepper. Toss in the onion, celery, carrots and bread. Allow the bread to soak up the liquid for about 10 minutes, giving it a stir every so often.

Carefully pull the hot cast iron from the oven and pour in the stuffing. Disperse the stuffing across the bottom of the pan so that it creates an even layer. Next, place the raw, seasoned pork chops on top of the stuffing so that they are not overlapping.

Return the pan filled with all its goodies back into the hot oven and bake for 35 minutes or until golden brown. Serve hot. If there are any leftovers, remove them from the cast iron.

BONELESS PORK CHOPS *with* BLACKBERRY JAM

This recipe is quick and easy with few ingredients, and the blackberry jam is nice and sweet with a bright acidity—it takes me back to my childhood. In the South, blackberries are everywhere. They are easy to find, easy to pick and even easier to eat. In lots of my neighbors' backyards, the plants seemed to form a jungle among the honeysuckles. I encourage you to take look at what types of edible plants are all around you. I'm not saying you've got to match the foraging style of chef René Redzepi, but you could give it a try.

SERVES 4

4 (½-inch [13-mm]-thick) boneless pork chops

1 tsp chopped fresh rosemary

1 tsp salt

1 tsp freshly cracked black pepper

2 tbsp (28 g) butter

BLACKBERRY JAM

8 oz (228 g) fresh blackberries

1 tbsp (15 ml) bourbon

½ cup (96 g) sugar

¼ cup (60 ml) freshly squeezed lemon juice

1 tsp salt

Season the pork chops with the rosemary, salt and pepper. Melt the butter on the stovetop over medium heat, then sear the chops 5 minutes on the first side and 4 minutes on the other side. Let the pork chops rest.

In a small saucepan over medium heat, cook the blackberries, bourbon, sugar, lemon juice and salt until the mixture is thick and candy-like, about 15 to 20 minutes. I like how rustic this sauce is. When you use the best ingredients, they get a chance to sing. You don't have to play the "I didn't buy quality ingredients" cover-up game. Less is more.

Serve the pork chops hot and covered in the blackberry jam.

BACON, LETTUCE *and* TOMATO RYE WRAP

Have you ever noticed how hard it is to eat a classic BLT on the go? For example, can you imagine eating a BLT while you drive your car to an important business meeting in your best outfit? Nah, I didn't think so. I'm changing that. I'm tired of not being able to enjoy a BLT while I run errands or ride my bike. This twist on a classic sandwich will leave you wondering what else you can do while you eat a BLT. For starters, I use cold leftover hollandaise as a substitute for mayo. Delicious.

SERVES 4

1 lb (455 g) applewood-smoked bacon, cut into cubes

All-natural maple syrup, to taste

1 cup (22 g) blackberry jam

Freshly cracked black pepper, to taste

Fresh parsley, to taste

1 lemon, zested

RYE WRAP

3 tbsp (42 g) butter

1 tbsp (8 g) caraway seeds

4 pieces store-bought naan bread

¼ cup (60 ml) Hollandaise (page 111), chilled

1 ripe tomato, cut into thin slices and seasoned with salt and freshly cracked black pepper

1 head iceberg lettuce, leaves torn as needed or any other crisp lettuce such as boston bibb, romaine, red leaf or belgian endive

Preheat the oven to 325°F (163°C). Line a shallow baking dish or a sheet tray with either foil or parchment paper and lay out the bacon cubes so they are barely touching. Drizzle them with the maple syrup, blackberry jam and season them with the pepper and parsley. Garnish with fresh lemon zest. Cook the bacon in the oven for 15 minutes if you like your bacon the texture of beef jerky. It works great, I promise.

To make the rye wrap, combine the butter and caraway seeds until they form a solid mixture. Spread the butter onto one side of the naan. Toast the naan in a cast iron skillet over medium heat, buttered-side down, for 5 minutes or until golden. (If you don't have a cast iron skillet, you can toast the naan on a baking sheet in a preheated 350°F [177°C] oven until it's golden.) You are multitasking here! The caraways seeds are toasting away while also crisping the naan. I only toast one side of the naan, which will be the side you start building your BLT on.

With the toasted side of the naan facing you, start building your sandwich. Give the wrap a nice smear of the Hollandaise. Next, place 3 slices of seasoned tomato. Now it's time for some pieces of chewy bacon. Last but not least, add a piece of lettuce. Tuck under a portion of the naan wrap and fold it like a burrito.

Tightly wrap up the sandwich in parchment paper. Enjoy now or later.

BRIOCHE, SAUSAGE *and* EGG BRUNCH BOMB

Breakfast is one of my favorite meals of the day, besides dessert. Well, duh. I love to play around with old school classics and try to reinvent the wheel. Here's a great example: think of that old school "eggs in a basket" dish where you place a cracked egg inside a piece of bread that has a circle cut out of its center. OK, now replace the bread with some spicy breakfast sausage. What?! Yep, that's a thing. Don't worry about flipping it over in a pan, this recipe takes all the hard work out of it for you. We're gonna bake this brunch bomb in the oven!

If you really wanna go the extra mile I suggest getting out the ol' mixer and dough hook for this amazing brioche recipe. Brioche is the butteriest of all the breads, but don't tell croissants that.

When you combine these two recipes, you're putting your best foot forward and you haven't even left the house yet.

SERVES 2

1 tsp active dry yeast

2 tbsp (30 ml) warm water (110°F [43°C])

1 tsp granulated sugar

1¼ cups (313 g) all-purpose flour

1 tsp salt

2 eggs

7 oz (198 g) butter, divided

EGG WASH

1 egg yolk

1 tbsp (15 ml) warm water (110°F [43°C])

RISE 'N' SHINE SAUSAGE

1 lb (455 g) ground pork

¼ cup (60 ml) orange juice

1 tsp dried sage

1 tsp red chili flakes

1 tbsp (15 ml) maple syrup

1 tsp freshly cracked black pepper

1 tsp salt

4 eggs

Preheat the oven to 400°F (204°C).

Activate the yeast by combining it with the warm water and sugar in a medium measuring cup. Let science run its course for about 10 minutes as the mixture becomes creamy on the top. In the bowl of a stand mixer, stir together the flour and salt. Make a little crater in the flour and add the activated yeast mixture and the eggs in the center of the crater. With a dough hook, beat the brioche until it has pulled together, away from the sides of the bowl.

Take the dough from the bowl and let it rest on a floured surface. I like to put a piece of plastic wrap or parchment paper in a jelly roll pan to help keep my flour mess to a minimum while it's resting.

With the dough flattened out, add 6 ounces (170 g) of the butter slowly while kneading the dough until it's all incorporated. Grease the jelly roll pan and an equivalent-size piece of plastic wrap with the remaining 1 ounce (28 g) of butter. Return the dough to the jelly roll pan once it has been buttered. Cover the dough with buttered plastic wrap and let the dough rise for 30 minutes in a nice warm spot in your kitchen.

Once it's doubled in size, punch the dough down and release any air left in it. Make the egg wash by combining the egg yolk with the warm water in a small bowl. Cut the dough into 4 pieces and brush them each with the egg wash. Let the dough pieces rise on the jelly roll pan one more time—they will double in size. Then pop them into your oven for 20 minutes.

To make the Rise 'N' Shine sausage, mix the ground pork with the orange juice, sage, red chili flakes, maple syrup, pepper and salt. Form the sausage into 4 patties. Place them on a jelly roll pan. In the middle of the patties, form a little well with your fingers for the cracked eggs (do this like you would make a pinch pot out of clay). I've tried several times to create an "egg in a basket" with a whole egg inside a sausage patty on the stovetop with no luck. So it's best to bake the patties in the oven on a jelly roll pan tray for 20 minutes at 400°F (204°C). I usually bake these patties with the brioche. Place a sausage patty in a freshly sliced roll of brioche and enjoy.

ROOT BEER BITES

I'm always looking for an excuse to buy root beer. I try not to drink it a lot, but it's the one thing other than bourbon I can't help myself to. Luckily it goes great with bacon, but what doesn't? I love this quick and easy preparation because I get my root beer fix while making a dish that goes with just about anything. I mean, you can even put these on top of a burger or add as a baked potato topper. The possibilities are endless.

SERVES 6

1-lb (454-g) piece of slab bacon, such as Nueske's applewood smoked bacon, cut into 1-inch (25-mm) cubes (if you can't find this style of bacon in one large chunk, smoked ham or smoked pork chops will work great also)

1 (12-oz [355-ml]) bottle of root beer, such as Barq's

In a medium or large saucepan, place the cubes of bacon down in a cold pan. Slowly bring the pan up to medium heat. When you are cooking things that have an ample amount of fat, the goal is to render the fat, not sear it. When you render the fat versus cooking it quickly with a high-heat sear, you actually develop a better crust and color as an end result.

As it cooks, the bacon will create fat to cook itself in. There is no need to add oil or butter to this, unless you're on a reverse diet, then by all means go for it. Sear all sides of the bacon on medium heat for about 5 minutes on each side.

Once the bacon chunks have reached your desired level of browning, pour off most of the residual fat that's been rendered. You can save it in a sealed container for weeks in the fridge, if you wish. I love to cook Bourbon-ana Bread Pudding (page 180) in it, in case you were curious.

Bring the pan back to the heat with most of the fat removed and pour in the root beer. Bring the pan to medium heat and let the root beer reduce by half or heat until it becomes syrupy in texture. Serve hot. This can be a great leftover if kept in the fridge in a sealed container for up to 3 days. If you want to reheat it, I would just bake it in a preheated oven of 350°F (177°C) for up to 15 minutes.

Chapter 3

DON'T BE A CHICKEN, BUY THE WHOLE BIRD:

～ Fowl ～

I will never understand why people don't buy whole chickens more often. The last time I checked, a whole bird's got something on it for everyone, whether it's dark meat or light meat. Buying the whole bird costs a lot less and it allows you the freedom to do with it what you choose.

BREAKING DOWN THE BIRD

When you break down a whole chicken for the first time, you will feel a sense of "wow, that wasn't really that bad."
All you need is a sharp knife—and this book.

SERVES 4

1 whole chicken (3- to 4-lb [1.4- to 1.8-kg])

Remove the chicken from the bag. Allow any excess liquid to go down the drain or into the sink. Set the little clucker down as if it's reading a book, sitting on its behind facing away from you.

Firmly hold its wing on your left and start to run your chef's knife straight down the right side of its back.

You will most likely find there is a bit of resistance at the end of this move once you hit the thigh bone. Keep going. That's why you need a nice, sturdy knife.

Remove the rest of the back by re-creating the same cutting action on the opposite side. Save the chicken back for stock.

At this point, you can open up the chicken. Some recipes call for a butterflied chicken. That is what you have now. Keep going.

With a solid stroke from the knife cut, the chicken will be in two parts, separated in half. You can cut down the breasts and between the thighs. You will find that close to where the neck used to be lives a wish bone that you can remove before or after you separate the chicken in two.

Next, remove the whole legs, starting from the thighs. You must separate the thighs from the lower abdomen. If you can't find where this intersection lies, I suggest breaking the bone out of the socket until you can get a feel for where that bone ends and begins. I didn't say saving money on chicken would be so glamorous. I've used the same method on chicken wings. I eventually figured it out and so will you.

Fresh, whole chicken, giblets removed. Not frozen.

Remove the backbone in a downward motion. Start to cut along one side of the backbone with a sharp knife, such as a chef's knife.

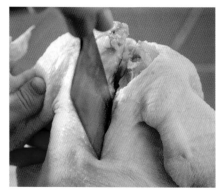

You will hear a crunching noise as your knife works its way down the first side of the chicken's spine.

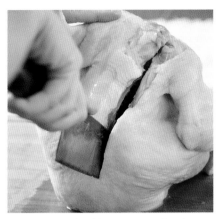

This part trips up a lot of first timers. You will need to apply more force as you wedge the knife through the thigh. Keep going, you're almost through the hardest part!

Congratulations, you have officially removed one side of the backbone from the chicken.

Repeat steps 3 through 6 with the other side. Save the back and keel bones from step 9 for stock.

Locate the keel bone, which separates the chicken breasts down the center of the bird. Give its top a tap with a sharp knife to gently expose the bone.

Start to remove the keel bone by running your fingers along the sides of it.

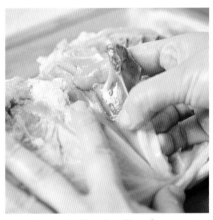

Remove the entire keel bone by pulling it from its top to its tapered bottom, toward the chicken's legs.

Remove the leg and thigh portion. You can easily do this by popping the thigh bone out of its sockets with your own two hands. Rawr. Once you have established where those joints used to meet, give it a nice whack with a sharp knife. Use this technique for removing the leg from the thigh too.

Use the tip in step 10 to remove the wing from the breast.

Cut up chicken—your finished product!

CITRUS SALT-ENCRUSTED CHICKEN

I had a fellow female butcher make this for me one night for dinner. I thought she was crazy—turns out she was brilliant. The salt crust pulls the lemon's zesty essence through its delicate meat, all the way to the crispy skin, resulting in a flavorful, juicy bird. No brine needed here!

SERVES 4

1 (3- to 4-lb [1.4- to 1.8-kg]) whole chicken

3 lemons, cut in half

8 to 10 cloves garlic, peeled

1 (3-lb [2-kg]) box kosher salt

Preheat the oven to 350°F (177°C). Stuff the chicken's cavity with the lemons and garlic. Place the stuffed chicken in a Dutch oven.

Cover the whole chicken in the salt and roast it in the oven for 35 minutes or until its internal temperature reads 160°F (71°C).

Once you remove the Dutch oven from the oven, gently remove the chicken from the Dutch oven. Peel away the salty skin to expose a silky, rich interior of lemon-flavored deliciousness. Discard the skin and the salt. Refrigerate any leftovers for up to 2 days.

FAUX SMOKED CHICKEN

We all have lazy day days, right? I'm a big believer in taking it easy on yourself in the kitchen from time to time. This recipe will make your taste buds think you fired up the smoker. But you know the truth. Behold, the Faux Smoked Chicken.

SERVES 4

5 tbsp (35 g) smoked paprika

1 tbsp (15 g) salt

1 tsp freshly cracked black pepper

1 tbsp (14 g) packed brown sugar

1 (3- to 4-lb [1.4- to 1.8-kg]) whole chicken

Preheat the oven to 350°F (177°C).

In a small bowl, combine the smoked paprika, salt, pepper and brown sugar. Cover the chicken in the dry rub. Place the chicken in a baking dish. Roast for 30 minutes or until an internal temperature of 160°F (71°C) has been reached.

PEPPERED "PASTRAMI"

I am willing to do anything to get people to stop buying processed lunch meat. I find this recipe to be reminiscent of turkey pastrami, of which I've sliced hundreds of pounds. Pastrami is known for its sharp peppery flavor, hidden behind a dark bark of fiery crust.

SERVES 4

4 tbsp (56 g) butter, at room temperature

6 tbsp (90 g) freshly cracked black pepper

2 tbsp (15 g) salt

1 (3- to 4-lb [1.4- to 1.8-kg]) whole chicken

Preheat the oven to 350°F (177°C).

Prepare the infused butter by taking room-temperature butter and cream in the black pepper and salt until combined. It will be easier to deal with when it is a nice creamy consistency. Set aside. Take the whole chicken and set it in a baking dish. The bird should be breast-side up with its legs facing you. Start to gently work your fingers underneath the skin. You will be creating a buttery, spicy layer under it.

With the soft butter in hand, place several tablespoons under the skin. In the areas where your fingers can't reach, you can smooth around the butter under the skin. Flip the bird over and repeat the same procedure until you are out of butter.

Roast the chicken breast-side up for 30 minutes or until it has reached an internal temperature of 160°F (71°C). Pull the baking dish out of the oven and allow the chicken to cool for 10 minutes. Remove the skin if you want to. I like to shred the meat from this recipe and refrigerate it for lunch meat during the week. It stays fresh for up to 3 days.

CHICKEN POT PIE

When I feel homesick or I'm having a bad day, and there's no one around to hug, I go for Chicken Pot Pie. It's the type of food that hugs you back. This is a low-stress recipe, where you can even use store-bought pie dough. With its flaky crust and silky chicken stock sauce, it's sure to be the thing that cures whatever ales ya. It has a ton of vegetables in it, so not only does is make you feel good, it's actually good for you. I haven't figured out a recipe for a chicken pot pie salad yet; I'm still working on it. Lol.

MAKES 1 (9-INCH [23-CM]) PIE

½ white onion, small dice

2 stalks celery, small dice

2 large carrots, small dice

½ lb (228 g) boneless, skinless chicken thighs, cut into 1-inch (2.5-cm) chunks

4 tbsp (56 g) butter

3 tbsp (23 g) all-purpose flour

4 cups (960 ml) chicken stock

1 tsp chopped fresh sage

1 tbsp (3 g) fresh thyme leaves

1 tsp cumin

2 tbsp (6 g) chopped fresh parsley

1 tsp red chili flakes

1 tsp salt

1 tsp freshly cracked black pepper

2 store-bought frozen pie crusts, thawed

EGG WASH

1 egg yolk

2 tbsp (30 ml) milk

Preheat the oven to 350°F (177°C).

Cook the onion, celery, carrots and chicken in the butter in a pie pan over medium heat. Once the veggies and chicken pieces have become slightly brown, sprinkle in the flour so that it can begin to thicken and form a roux, which will make the sauce.

Add the chicken stock, sage, thyme, cumin, parsley, red chili flakes, salt and pepper and bring the mixture to a simmer. Pour this mixture directly into one of the pie crusts. Cover the top of the Chicken Pot Pie with the second pie crust and crease it to the rim of the first pie crust.

Mix together the egg yolk and milk in a small bowl to create the egg wash and brush it on the crusts before baking the pot pie in the oven for 35 minutes. Let the pot pie rest and thicken up for 15 minutes before serving. This dish may also be frozen and baked at a later date.

CHICKEN IN A DUMPLING

I thought it would be fun to do a whimsical play of one of my favorite dishes of all-time: chicken and dumplings. I take the chilled leftovers from the Chicken Pot Pie on page 85 and encase it in a savory pie dough. The dumpling then gets pan fried and is served hot. This preparation is reminiscent of pierogies and results in a more chewy dumpling versus deep frying. It's also healthier.

SERVES 2

2 eggs

1 tbsp (15 g) salt

2 cups (480 ml) milk

4 cups (1 kg) all-purpose flour

1 bunch fresh parsley, finely chopped

1 batch Chicken Pot Pie filling (page 85)

2 tbsp (30 ml) vegetable oil

Combine the eggs, salt and milk in a medium bowl. Place the flour in another medium bowl and create the dumpling dough by drizzling the egg mixture into the center of the flour. With a fork, gently start marrying the wet and dry mixtures. Eventually, the dough will not want to stick to the sides of the bowl and at that point you will start kneading it with your hands on a floured surface.

Sprinkle the parsley over the dough and knead by hand until it's nice and tough. Cut the dough out on the countertop after rolling it out about ½-inch (13-mm) thick. You can use a large round cup or a small bowl with sharp edges if you don't have a cutter. You can make these stuffed dumplings any shape you want as long as they are filled with the Chicken Pot Pie filling. I like to create recipes that allow wiggle room for self-expression.

Once you cut the dough into the desired shapes, take a bit of water on your finger and run it along one side of the dough piece. You don't want any holes or leaks. Once you drop a portion of the chicken mixture onto the dough, this small swipe of moisture will help you close it properly. I often pick my dumplings up off the well-floured counter to be sure I'm sealing them properly. These can be made up ahead of time and even frozen for future use. As long as they don't get freezer burnt, they will last for months when frozen.

Heat the vegetable oil over medium heat in a large, heavy-bottomed pan. Sear each side of the dumplings until golden brown. Serve hot. These also hold well in the oven after being browned in the pan.

Roll out the chilled dough onto a lightly floured surface and cut out the circles.

Fill the dough circles with the stuffing and fold in half. Use water around the rims as an adhesive.

Make several indentations with a fork, ensuring there won't be any leaks.

These darker, silkier parts of the chicken are my favorite. When I was younger, I was tricked into thinking that they weren't as good as white meat. For years, I was stuck in an all-white-meat time warp. If you don't think you like dark meat, I invite you to try it again. The following recipes were designed for success whether you're cooking wings, thighs, legs or whole quarters. The only adjustment that need be made to the recipes is cooking time. Consult the following table for guidance on how long to cook each part of the bird:

SUGGESTED COOKING TIMES FOR AN OVEN AT 350°F (177°C)	
Wings	15 minutes (broil wings)
Thighs (bone in, skin on)	20 minutes
Thighs (boneless, skinless)	15 minutes
Legs (bone in, skin on)	15 minutes
Whole Leg Quarters (bone in, skin on)	17 minutes

BOURBON BARBECUE WINGS *with* FIG GASTRIQUE

Let's be real here. Bourbon makes just about everything better. Its luscious smokiness riddled with hints of brown sugar are the type of flavors that can make you melt right into your chair. Now add some chicken wings to the mix and you're set for any game day celebration.

But wait, what's a *gastrique*? Basically it's a style of sauce that's got a punch of vinegar with a finish of sweetness. The last time I checked, those are the flavors of a perfect barbecue sauce! The texture of the sauce is like honey, cuz it will stick to anything. This style of sauce is for those who love a nice sweet flavor profile, also known as a crowd pleaser. If you don't lick your fingers, someone else will! I am positive you'll find the flavor of fig to your liking and wouldn't be surprised if it became a staple in your kitchen.

SERVES 4

3 lb (1.4 kg) chicken wings

1 cup (240 ml) bourbon

1 cup (220 g) packed brown sugar

1 tbsp (15 g) salt

1 bunch scallions, thinly sliced, for garnish

FIG GASTRIQUE

1 jar prepared fig preserves

2 tbsp (30 ml) bourbon

1 tsp red chili flakes

Preheat the oven to broil.

Toss the wings in the bourbon, brown sugar and salt and broil them on a sheet tray for 15 minutes. Halfway through the cooking process, flip the wings.

In a small saucepan, combine the fig preserves, bourbon and red chili flakes until well-incorporated. Serve the sauce warm with the wings. Garnish the wings with the scallions.

PIZZA WINGS *with* HERBED BUTTERMILK AND CELERY PICKLES

This might be the best chicken wing creation ever. I felt it necessary to incorporate two fantastic bar bites—pizza and wings—into one! Can it be done? Of course it can! The tangy herbed buttermilk flavor is the perfect sidekick to these pizza wings. You no longer have to pick between your favorite bar food staples. Don't worry, I didn't forget about the celery. Its crispy pickled stalks are the perfect palate cleanser.

SERVES 3

6 oz (170 g) thinly sliced pepperoni

8 oz (227 g) grated Parmesan cheese

3 cups (720 ml) tomato sauce (see recipe on page 109) or store-bought tomato sauce, warmed

1 bunch fresh basil

3 lb (1.4 kg) chicken wings

HERBED BUTTERMILK

1 cup (228 g) sour cream

2 tbsp (14 g) nutritional yeast or tahini paste

Juice of 1 lemon

1 tsp fresh oregano, minced

1 tsp fresh dill, minced

1 tsp fresh parsley, minced

Salt and freshly cracked black pepper, to taste

CELERY PICKLES

4 large stalks celery, washed, split down the middle and cut into quarters

1 cup (240 ml) white wine vinegar

1 cup (240 ml) cold water

In a large bowl, mix together the cut pieces of pepperoni, grated cheese, tomato sauce and basil. Add the chicken wings and toss until they are completely covered. Place on a baking dish so that they are not touching.

To make the herbed buttermilk, mix the sour cream, nutritional yeast, lemon juice, oregano, dill, parsley and salt and pepper together in a large bowl until smooth. Keep refrigerated until needed. If kept cold in a sealed container, the sauce will be good for a week.

To make the celery pickles, combine the celery, white wine vinegar and cold water in a large mason jar. Serve cold. This refreshing celery is good for 2 days when kept in the pickling liquid. Remove the celery from the liquid before serving. The liquid can be saved for another refrigerator pickle, salad dressing or meat brine.

After prepping the wings for the oven, drizzle the warm tomato sauce on them and broil them for 15 minutes. You won't need to flip the wings for this recipe during the cooking process. Serve the wings hot out of the oven with fresh basil, herbed buttermilk and celery pickles.

LOUISIANA-STYLE WINGS
with SMOKY BLUE CHEESE SAUCE

There's absolutely nothing wrong with the classics. This recipe is straight to the point. That iconic vinegar-based Southern heat, known as "Louisiana-style," is a crowd pleaser. It's not too spicy and not too mild. The smoked blue cheese sauce really knocks this soon-to-be favorite out of the park.

SERVES 3

3 lb (1.4 kg) chicken wings

1 (12-oz [340-ml]) bottle hot sauce
(I prefer Crystal brand)

½ cup (120 ml) bourbon

SMOKY BLUE CHEESE SAUCE

8 oz (184 g) smoked blue cheese

8 oz (228 g) sour cream

1 bunch scallions, root ends trimmed

Marinate the wings in the hot sauce and bourbon overnight or up to 2 days in the fridge. Lay the wings in a baking dish completely covered in the sauce.

Preheat the oven to 350°F (177°C). While the oven preheats, make the smoky blue cheese sauce. In a food processor, mix the smoked blue cheese, sour cream and scallions until smooth. The flavor of this sauce is as memorable as your first trip to Louisiana. I love how it turns a unique color of green. Scallions are so delicious. Serve cold. Keep the sauce refrigerated for up to 2 weeks.

Bake the wings for 20 to 25 minutes. Serve them hot with a side of smoky blue cheese sauce.

BUTTERNUT THIGHS

The best dishes hit a variety of flavor profiles. You've got the sweet, salty, spicy, herbal and buttery ones all in one place with this one. It's got a real country vibe to it, like you've been cooking it all day, but we know it took less than an hour. I love how quick and easy it is to enjoy butternut squash this way. For years, I toiled with peeling and dicing them . . . Not anymore!

SERVES 4

1 tbsp (7 g) dry mustard

2 tbsp (14 g) Cajun seasoning

2 lb (910 g) bone-in, skin-on chicken thighs

2 medium butternut squash, cut in half, seeds removed

2 tbsp (6 g) chopped fresh sage

4 tbsp (56 g) butter

AROMATIC LIQUID

3 large bell peppers

1 large onion, cut into 4 pieces

2 stalks celery

2 tomatoes

Preheat the oven to 350°F (177°C).

Mix the dry mustard and Cajun seasoning together in a small bowl and cover all sides of the chicken thighs with the dry rub. This dry rub is a simple one but it's full of flavor without all the fuss. Bone-in, skin-on thighs are great because you can't really dry them out!

In a large cast iron pan over medium heat, place the chicken thighs skin-side down. This slow and mellow heat allows us to slowly render the fat of the chicken skin. Once the skin has reached a golden-brown state, it's a good time to flip the thighs over.

In a blender, combine the peppers, onion, celery and tomatoes and blend until smooth. Pour the aromatic liquid over the thighs and pop that pan into the oven. In about 40 minutes, your chicken is done and your wonderful broth has reduced to a beautiful state.

Lay out 4 pieces of foil big enough to wrap each piece of squash in. Since you have removed the seeds with a large spoon, there is a nice little cubby hole where you can place the sage and butter while the squash roasts in the oven. Place the squash flesh-side up on top of the foil. Last but not least, drizzle about 1 tablespoon (15 ml) water in the little cubby as it will aid in steaming the squash. Wrap the foil tightly around each individual piece and place them cubby hole–side down on a baking dish. If you put them in at the same time as the chicken thighs, they will be done at the same time. Serve hot. This dish makes great leftovers.

Serve the thighs and butternut squash together. Pour the pan sauce over them both.

BROWN PAPER BAG CHICKEN

The words "fried chicken" make people listen. The next time I'm talking to someone and they aren't paying attention,
I'm going to say those two magical words. Brown Paper Bag Chicken is all about doing it the old-school Southern way.
I'll show ya how! Just make sure that your brown paper bag doesn't have any holes in it. I made a huge mess one time.
You live, you learn. Actually, how 'bout we double-bag it this time?

SERVES 4

8 oz (228 g) sour cream

4 eggs

1 bunch fresh tarragon or parsley, chopped

1 whole chicken, cut into 8 pieces

8 cups (1.9 L) vegetable oil

DRY MIX

4 cups (1 kg) all-purpose flour

1 cup (151 g) cornstarch

2 tbsp (30 g) salt

2 tbsp (30 g) freshly cracked black pepper

2 tbsp (30 g) garlic salt

In a large bowl, mix together the sour cream, eggs and tarragon until they are combined. Add the chicken pieces to the mix and soak overnight if possible. If not, that's fine too. Make sure every nook and cranny of the chicken pieces are covered with tangy goodness.

Next, create the dry mix by combining the flour, cornstarch, salt, pepper and garlic salt in double-bagged brown paper bags. Give the bags a good toss to thoroughly incorporate all the ingredients.

Pour the vegetable oil into a large cast iron pot or Dutch oven and bring it up to 325°F (163°C). This is a good temperature to fry chicken. You will need to flip the pieces over halfway through cooking.

Now it's time to take the chicken pieces from the sour cream mixture and coat them in the breading. If you have a pair of chopsticks, it's a great time to use them. They work great for breading pretty much everything. If you don't have any, the second best thing is a fork.

First, carefully drop the breasts into the breading and give them a shake after you fold over the top of the bag. Take a peek inside to see just how covered they are. If they are covered in the flour, gently lay the breasts down in the oil. Next are the thighs, legs and wings. You want your chicken to be 160°F (71°C) internally when it's done cooking.

If you want to keep the chicken hot, just place it on a baking sheet in a 300°F (149°C) oven for up to 30 minutes. Fried chicken makes pretty good leftovers, but from my experience, there usually aren't any.

CRISPY CHICKEN SKIN, LETTUCE AND TOMATO SANDWICH *with* TARRAGON MAYO

There are people in this world who don't eat bacon or pork for one reason or another. Hopefully, those people happen to enjoy chicken. I created this sandwich for those people, because deep down I'm pretty sure they miss the bacon. If not, they can just enjoy a tomato and lettuce sandwich.

MAKES 2 SANDWICHES

8 oz (228 g) raw chicken skin

1 tsp salt

1 tsp freshly cracked black pepper

1 tsp olive oil

4 slices Texas toast

1 tomato, cut into thin slices and seasoned with salt and freshly cracked black pepper

1 small head iceberg lettuce, core removed

TARRAGON MAYO

2 egg yolks

4 tbsp (60 ml) olive oil

1 clove garlic, minced

Juice of 1 lemon

1 tbsp (3 g) fresh tarragon, minced

Salt and freshly cracked black pepper, to taste

Preheat the oven to 300°F (149°C). Season the chicken skin with the salt and pepper and place it on a baking sheet that has been smeared with the olive oil. Bake the chicken skin in the oven until golden brown and crispy, usually about 15 to 20 minutes. Ironically enough, the chicken skin can be treated like bacon. There is a fine line between nice and crispy and burnt. Keep an eye on it.

To make the tarragon mayo, whisk the egg yolks in a small bowl until frothy. Slowly add the oil in a thin, steady stream, 1 tablespoon (15 ml) at a time. This process can be sped up quickly by using a food processor. Once the egg yolks and olive oil are emulsified, they will start to appear like a traditional store-bought mayo, except more delicious. Add the garlic, lemon juice and tarragon. Season the mayo with salt and pepper. This can be stored in the fridge for up to 3 days. The fresh tarragon, or any other fresh herb, for that matter, makes it a lot more perishable. Keep the mayo refrigerated until ready to use.

Once the chicken skin is done rendering, remove it from the baking sheet and place it on a paper towel. Take the Texas toast and smear each slice around on the baking sheet so that they soak up the residual chicken fat. This natural fat acts as a "butter" to toast the bread. Place the Texas toast on the baking sheet and return the baking sheet to the oven and bake for an additional 5 minutes or until the desired color is developed on the toast.

Smear the tarragon mayo on both sides of the bread. Add a few slices of tomato and pieces of iceberg lettuce and top if off with a few pieces of chicken skin. You are now good to go.

Butcher Babe Tip

If you gradually start to save pieces of raw chicken skin from other cuts of chicken you purchase, you will quickly have enough to create this unique sandwich. I store my chicken skin in the freezer. I lay each piece between individual layers of plastic wrap; that way, they are easy to grab when I need them.

PERFECTLY POACHED POULTRY

Poaching is a cooking technique that involves a hot simmering liquid just below the boiling point. When you are poaching something, the liquid should be barely steaming. This is a great way to cook all-white-meat pieces of chicken because it won't dry out. This chicken is great as part of a green salad, sandwich or chicken salad. You can cook any type of poultry protein this way.

MAKES 2 LB (910 G) CHICKEN

2 tbsp (28 g; 30 ml) butter or olive oil

3 cloves garlic, minced

1 tomato, small dice

4 cups (960 ml) chicken stock or water

1 cup (240 ml) white wine

½ bunch fresh parsley

1 tsp salt

1 tsp freshly cracked black pepper

2 lb (910 g) chicken breasts, thighs, legs and wings (boneless, skinless chicken breasts cut into long 1-inch [2.5-cm] wide strips work great too)

Add the butter, garlic and tomato to the bottom of a saucepan over medium heat. Allow the garlic to become slightly brown. Add the chicken stock, wine and parsley. Heat this liquid to at least 180°F (82°C) but no higher than 190°F (88°C). Season with salt and pepper.

Add the larger pieces of chicken first so that they have the time to cook appropriately. I start with the breasts first, then the thighs and legs, and last, but not least, the wings. Cook the chicken completely, poaching for about 10 to 12 minutes or until they reach an internal temperature of 160°F (71°C).

Remove them from the poaching liquid and place them in a food storage container if you're planning on eating them chilled. Repeat this process until all the chicken is cooked. You can eat this poached chicken hot or cold. It lasts up to 3 days in the fridge.

HAVARTI SPINACH ROULADE

Classically speaking, a roulade is a dish made of rolled meats or pastry. In this case, the roulade you will be creating is composed of boneless, skinless chicken breast, sautéed spinach and Havarti cheese. I love this dish. It makes fantastic leftovers and can be made with a plethora of different flavor combinations.

SERVES 4

2 tbsp (28 g) butter

1½ lb (680 g) fresh spinach

1 red bell pepper, small dice, seeds removed

4 cloves garlic, minced

1 tsp red chili flakes

2 tbsp (30 ml) bourbon

¼ cup (60 ml) heavy whipping cream

4 boneless, skinless chicken breasts

2 tsp (10 g) salt

2 tsp (10 g) freshly cracked black pepper

6 thick slices of Havarti cheese (about a ½ lb [228 g])

2 tbsp (30 ml) olive oil (for browning roulades)

PAN SAUCE

1 cup (240 ml) white wine or bourbon

1 tomato, small dice

4 cloves garlic, minced

Preheat the oven to 325°F (163°C).

Melt the butter in a pan over high heat and cook the spinach, bell pepper, garlic, red chili flakes and bourbon for 5 minutes. Remove the pan from the heat and immediately add the heavy whipping cream. Allow the mixture to cool slightly on the stovetop while you prep the chicken breasts.

When I'm working with chicken, I like to cover my cutting board with plastic wrap so I can season the poultry without any worry that I could get raw chicken juice on anything in my kitchen. Place the chicken breasts so that the small pointed ends of the breasts are facing you. Season the breasts with salt and pepper. Place another piece of plastic wrap over the breasts so that they are completely covered.

You are now going to slightly flatten the chicken breasts with a kitchen pan. I find that a small saucepan works great. The trick is to whack the chicken dead center. After 3 or 4 swift pounds to the poultry, you should be ready to go. The shape and thickness of the chicken will now be more suitable for rolling into a roulade.

Remove the top layer of plastic wrap and place a few pieces of the Havarti on the chicken breasts. Place the spinach filling on top of the Havarti.

The trick now is rolling the chicken breasts. Beginning at the narrower end of the chicken, roll the breast away from you. Once you make a nice little snug roulade, tie it once with butcher's twine to secure the roll. If you can't get your hands on any twine, then just use a toothpick or wooden skewer, which are a lot trickier but will work in a pinch. Repeat this process until all the chicken breasts are tied and ready to go back into the pan used to cook the spinach filling.

Pour the olive oil into the pan on the stovetop and heat it over medium-high heat. Sear the roulades until all sides are golden brown. Place the pan into the oven and continue to bake for about 10 minutes or until the internal temperature reads 160°F (71°C).

Remove the roulades from the hot pan and place them on a cutting board to rest for about 10 minutes. Remove the string or toothpicks. While the roulades are resting, bring the pan back to the stovetop to make the pan sauce. All those yummy chicken drippings can't go to waste!

With the pan over medium-high heat, add the white wine, tomato and garlic and cook until the sauce reduces by half. Slice the roulades into 1-inch (2.5-cm) pieces with a sharp knife. Remove the pan from the heat. Pour the pan sauce over the sliced roulades. Serve immediately.

SPICY ANDOUILLE ROULADE *with* SMOKY CORN SAUTÉ

If you like chicken and smoked spicy sausage, this recipe is probably already calling your name. It's totally worth the effort to try and start flexing some of your new butchery skills because after all, you are reading *The Butcher Babe Cookbook*. Do you know what the "holy trinity" is? Basically, the holy trinity is a flavorful mix of bell peppers, celery and onions. When you get this dish cooking up in your home, it'll smell like the deep South.

SERVES 4

HOLY TRINITY FILLING

2 stalks celery, small dice

2 red bell peppers, cut into thin strips, seeds removed

1 sweet white onion, cut into thin strips

1 tbsp (14 g) butter

2 tbsp (30 ml) Dijon mustard

2 tbsp (30 ml) bourbon

2 tsp (10 g) celery salt

1 tbsp (7 g) dry mustard

1 tbsp (14 g) packed brown sugar

1 tsp salt

1 tsp freshly cracked black pepper

2 links (1 lb [455 g]) smoked andouille sausage

4 boneless, skinless chicken breast cutlets

SMOKY CORN SAUTÉ

1 (16-oz [455-g]) bag frozen corn

2 tbsp (28 g) butter

2 tbsp (14 g) smoked paprika

1 tbsp (15 ml) Louisiana-style hot sauce

1 tbsp (14 g) packed brown sugar

Salt and freshly cracked black pepper, to taste

1 bunch fresh scallions, thinly sliced on the bias, for garnish

Preheat the oven to 350°F (177°C).

In a pan over high heat, cook the celery, bell peppers, onion, butter, Dijon mustard and bourbon for 10 minutes. Remove the holy trinity filling from the heat.

Make the dry rub by combining the celery salt, mustard, brown sugar, salt and pepper in a small bowl. Set aside.

Cut the andouille sausages into thirds, cut those pieces in half lengthwise and set aside. Place a large piece of plastic wrap over a cutting board. Place the chicken cutlets down and season them with the dry rub on both sides. The smaller, tapered end of the cutlets should be facing you.

Place 4 strips of the andouille sausage on each cutlet. Portion the filling between the cutlets and start rolling from the smaller, tapered end of the chicken to the top of the breast. Tie the roulades with butcher's twine. Place the roulades in the pan the filling was made in and place it in the oven. Throw away the plastic wrap.

The roulade should cook for about 25 minutes or until the internal temperature has reached 160°F (71°C). Remove the roulades from the pan and place them on a cutting board. Let them rest for 10 minutes.

Place the pan that you cooked the roulades in back on the stovetop. Bring the pan up to high heat. Once the pan starts to sizzle, add the frozen corn, butter, smoked paprika, hot sauce and brown sugar. Cook, stirring frequently, for 10 minutes or until the corn is hot and steaming. Season the corn with salt and pepper. Remove the pan from the heat. Cut the ties from the chicken, then slice the roulade into 1-inch (2.5-cm) rounds. Serve the chicken on a bed of the corn. Garnish the dish with the scallions. Serve immediately. Makes great leftovers for up to 5 days in the fridge.

Add the filling to the chicken cutlets.

Close the roulade by trussing the chicken breast together.

CREAM CORN STUFFED CORNISH HENS

Cornish hens are a completely different breed of fowl. They are extremely small, about 1 pound (455 g) or so apiece. Cornish hens look just like little baby chickens and they taste about the same way. I think that are so fun to cook and serve individually to guests.

These little guys are stuffed with a quick and easy cornbread with a spicy surprise hidden inside!

Generally, you will only find these little hens frozen. So if you know you're going to want to serve them, you will need to think ahead about two days. The best way to thaw poultry is in the fridge, not under running water and most definitely not in the microwave. When you let a protein slowly thaw under refrigeration, it's called slacking.

SERVES 4

CORNBREAD STUFFING

1 (8½-oz [241-g]) box cornbread mix

½ cup (113 g) cream corn

¼ cup (38 g) diced celery

¼ cup (38 g) diced green pepper

CREAM CHEESE STUFFED JALAPEÑO

3 oz (85 g) cream cheese

1 tbsp (11 g) diced canned pimento, drained

¼ tsp garlic powder

1 tsp packed brown sugar

4 small jalapeños

4 Cornish hens, thawed

4 tbsp (56 g) butter, at room temperature

4 tbsp (28 g) Cajun seasoning

Preheat the oven to 350°F (177°C). Prepare the cornbread mix according to the package directions and add the cream corn, celery and green pepper. Bake the cornbread until just set in the center. Let cool.

In a small bowl, cream together the cream cheese, pimento, garlic powder and brown sugar. Carefully remove the tops from the jalapeños and remove the seeds. I use a butter knife to knock the seeds out. Fill the jalapeños with the cream cheese mixture until they are full. I use a butter knife for this part too. Set aside.

Let's assemble this dish! Stuff the uncooked Cornish hens with the cooked cornbread until they are half full. This can get a little messy. I stuff my birds over a stainless steel bowl.

When the hens are half full, place a stuffed jalapeño inside each bird. The point of this dish is to keep the jalapeño hidden, as a surprise. Now fill the rest of the cavity with the cornbread, letting some spill out. I love that this stuffing is already cooked, so I really just have to worry about the hens being the perfect doneness.

Rub the hens with the butter and then sprinkle the Cajun seasoning over them.

Place all 4 stuffed birds in a large cast iron pan, being careful that they aren't touching. Roast them in the oven for up to 1 hour or until the internal temperature reads 160°F (71°C). Serve immediately.

Bring the mini chicken legs together with some butcher's twine. Bringing them to the point where it's cross-legged makes it cook evenly so it won't dry out.

Butter, butter, butter. Sprinkle liberally with Cajun seasoning.

TINY TURDUCKEN

There is a certain amount of mystique surrounding the Southern classic, the "turducken." For good reason, many have marveled at the beautiful combination of turkey, duck and chicken. However amazing, the combination of the whole dish is larger than life. Not everyone has a crowd large enough to justify cooking a monster-sized 15-pound (7-kg) bird hybrid. So, I've adapted a recipe to create a smaller version. This is my version of the larger-than-life original. It might even fit in your lunch box. Maybe.

SERVES 6

1 (2- to 3-lb [907- to 1,360-g]) whole turkey breast, bones removed

1 lb (454 g) boneless skinless chicken thighs

2 (1-lb [454-g]) duck breasts

BIRD RUB

4 tbsp (30 g) smoked paprika

1 bunch fresh thyme, leaves only

3 tbsp (45 g) smoked salt (if you can't find smoked, regular is fine)

2 tbsp (12 g) ground black pepper

3 tbsp (27 g) light brown sugar

½ cup (118 ml) Dijon mustard

Preheat the oven to 300°F (150°C). On a large cutting board, carefully remove the skin from the turkey breast and set it aside. You will use this to 'bard' the roast before it gets baked. Bard means to wrap in fat, more or less.

With a sharp knife, butterfly the turkey breast down the middle horizontally, so that it becomes open into one piece. The breast needs to be in one piece. In a small mixing bowl, mix together the bird rub. Spread the rub all over the turkey breast, chicken thighs and duck breasts, so all parts of the roast will be seasoned.

Place the chicken thighs in the center of the turkey breasts so that they are not overlapping one another. Last but not least, place one of the duck breasts on one of the sides of turkey breast and thighs. Bring the pieces together, essentially 'closing' a book made of types of fowl. Fold any piece of meat under and tuck them inside the roast you are about to roll and tie with butcher's twine.

Start from the center and tie it nice and taught. Clip any trimmings. I tie mine about 1 inch (2.5 cm) apart from one another. Tie a few butcher ties opposite from the ones you did previously. Place the roast in a large pan, such as a Dutch oven or a baking dish with sides.

Smear on the remaining bird rub and place in the oven. Bake until the duck breasts that are nestled in the center of the roast have reached an internal temperature of 135°F (58°C). They should be a nice medium temperature with a slight amount of pink to them. If you like well-done duck, then cook it longer. This will take about 2 hours.

Remove the roast from the oven and let it rest for 15 minutes. Remove the ties with kitchen scissors or a sharp knife and slice. I slice mine into 2-inch (5-cm) pieces, and serve hot.

Reheat in the oven for leftovers for 15 minutes on 350°F (177°C). Also makes great sandwiches, if you let it chill overnight and slice it very thinly with a sharp knife. This roast is good for up to 4 days.

Chapter 4

BUTTER AND BONES, A CLASSICAL APPROACH:
Sauces

There are a few things that you need to know how to do in order to be a confident cook. One of those things is learning how to make sauces. Making sauces, in my opinion, is basically just science in motion. Once you learn the scientific laws that rule the culinary world, you can break them.

While we are discussing things you need to know, let me remind you that every great cook out there has burnt an innumerable amount of things in their lifetime. Every great cook has thrown away hours of work because there were no ways to fix that mistake, or perhaps they were not aware of them.

The following kitchen hacks are designed to make you more confident in the kitchen. Trust me, I learned the hard way for you already.

Whoops I...

1. Burnt the bottom of the pan
Stop what you are doing and take the pan off of the heat. For some reason a lot of cooks go into panic mode and start to stir the sauce or soup with the desperation of 1000 sinking ships. That's your first mistake. Leave the burnt bits in the bottom of the pan. Transfer the liquid to another pan, and begin again. You may have to also strain the liquid while transferring it depending on its viscosity.

2. Have lumps in my sauce
This happens a lot. It's generally an easy fix, involving a mesh strainer. Just filter out those little floury bits and keep on moving. Lumps in sauces happen when the roux isn't made properly. One must always use a wooden spoon in the sauce-making realm. Wooden spoons allow you to feel the bottom of your pans with out burning your finger tips off. Very cool.

3. Broke my sauce
Dinner's ruined! A broken sauce can be brought back to life no problem. Got a blender? Got a whisk? There you go. If your hollandaise is too thick, slowly add hot water. If your hollandaise is too thin, add some more acid, such as hot sauce, vinegar or lemon juice. The acidity of these ingredients binds to the fat (butter and egg yolks) and slightly cooks the two, creating a luscious viscosity.

BÉCHAMEL

This creamy white sauce is made from milk and a roux. This sauce is easily turned into
a cheese sauce for various favorites such as mac 'n' cheese.

MAKES 1 ½ CUPS (355 ML)

2 tbsp (28 g) butter

2 tbsp (16 g) flour

1¼ cups (300 ml) milk, heated just until it
starts to simmer

Freshly cracked white pepper, to taste

In a saucepan, cook together the butter and the flour over medium-low heat until light brown
in color. This is one of the most important things you will master in your kitchen. The best
tool for this is a flat-bottomed wooden spoon and a whisk. It's kind of like making children's
modeling compound.

Roux can be created in a variety of colors. The darker the roux, the less thickening power it has.

Once the roux has developed some color, whisk in the hot milk and white pepper. Maintain a
heat of medium-low so that you will not burn the liquid.

ESPAGNOLE

Also known as brown sauce, espagnole can ultimately be turned into demi-glace. I often refer to demi-glace
as meat caramel. It's thick and hearty and pairs well with all varieties of red meat.

MAKES 1 QUART (945 ML)

½ cup (75 g) large onion, diced

¼ cup (38 g) large whole carrots, diced

¼ cup (38 g) whole celery (not hearts), diced

2 tbsp (28 g) butter

2 tbsp (16 g) all-purpose flour

2 tbsp (30 g) tomato paste

3 cups (720 ml) stock (see page 118)

1 dried bay leaf

1 tbsp (2.5 g) fresh parsley

Dash freshly cracked black pepper

Cook the onion, carrots and celery in the butter on medium heat until they are lightly browned.
Slowly sprinkle the flour into the pan with the browned mirepoix and form a roux. Cook this
roux much longer on medium heat so that a richer color develops. After the dark brown roux is
formed, add the tomato paste and mix until smooth with a wooden spoon. If there are still lumps,
just use a whisk.

Slowly add the stock to the roux while whisking vigorously. Once all the stock is added to the
pan, add the bay leaf, parsley and pepper. Reduce the liquid by one-third over medium heat.
This will take about 30 minutes. Strain the liquid before serving. Espagnole can be made ahead
of time and frozen in ice cube trays for general use.

TOMATO SAUCE

Lucky for you, there's no need to even get out a knife. I'm mixing the old with the new here. The best classical tomato sauce, or red sauce, recipes always call for pork neck bones. If you are unable to find any, baby back bones work fine too.

MAKES 4 QUARTS (3.7 L)

5 to 6 lb (2.3 to 2.7 kg) tomatoes, unpeeled

1 cup (240 ml) olive oil

2 cups (480 ml) red wine

1 cup (240 ml) red wine vinegar

1 cup (240 ml) balsamic vinegar or ½ cup (72 g) brown sugar

10 cloves garlic

1 white onion, skin and root removed

3 lb (1.3 kg) pork neck bones

1 bunch fresh oregano leaves

1 bunch fresh thyme leaves

Place the tomatoes, olive oil, red wine, red wine vinegar, balsamic vinegar, garlic and onion in a food processor and blend until smooth. (You may have to cut the veggies a little bit to help the food processor do its job.)

Add the puréed liquid and pork bones to a Dutch oven over medium heat and let the mixture reduce for several hours. Remove the bones after it's done cooking, then add the oregano and thyme.

This sauce does wonderful in the freezer for months at a time. Simply wait until the sauce is cool and store it in airtight plastic bags or containers.

HOLLANDAISE

This liaison of butter and egg yolks is so wonderful. It's hands down my favorite sauce. I could drink it. For real.

MAKES 2 CUPS (473 ML)

10 oz (284 g) butter

1 clove garlic

6 egg yolks

4 tbsp (60 ml) freshly squeezed lemon juice

1 tbsp (15 ml) distilled white vinegar

1 tbsp (15 ml) Louisiana-style hot sauce

Salt and freshly cracked black pepper, to taste

Bring the butter and garlic to a simmer on the stovetop.

In a food processor, purée the egg yolks until frothy. This usually takes about 5 minutes.

Very slowly pour the hot butter into the food processor with the egg yolks. You can hear the hollandaise thicken up as more butter is added. It's good to keep some warm water handy in case this sauce starts to thicken too much on you. Just add the warm water, 1 tablespoon (15 ml) at time if need be.

Finish the sauce by adding the lemon juice, vinegar and hot sauce. Season with salt and pepper and enjoy. This stuff could make dirt taste good. I never throw this sauce away if there are leftovers. It's a great substitute for mayo.

Checking to see if the sauce is the right viscosity, or consistency. Classically, using the back of a spoon is the best way to tell how thick or thin a sauce is.

This sauce has a nape texture. Nape means that the sauce is thick enough to stick to the spoon and hold a line drawn by your finger, as well as lightly coating food with a thin, even layer.

VOLUTE

This sauce is easy as can be. It's essentially the flavors of a chicken pot pie in a sauce. Classically speaking, this sauce is of the white variety just like a béchamel and it's just as versatile. You can use a variety of stocks and take the sauce in hundreds of directions.

MAKES 3 CUPS (710 ML)

3 cups (720 ml) chicken stock

1 oz (28 g) butter

1 oz (28 g) all-purpose flour

Bring the chicken stock to a simmer in a saucepan, making sure to keep it hot on the stovetop.

Meanwhile, in a heavy-bottomed saucepan, combine the butter and flour for a blonde roux. Once the butter and flour are combined and form a paste, it has the power to transform any liquid into a luscious sauce.

Slowly pour the hot chicken stock into the roux while whisking quickly. Try not to get any lumps in the volute. If you happen to get lumps, you can just strain them out.

Chapter 5

ON THE GRIND:
~ Culinary Concepts in Frugality ~

The art of turning nothing into something.

It blows my mind every year what we throw away. More often than not, I have had feelings of guilt as I toted my heavy garbage bag out to the trashcan. I was left wondering what I didn't do right and how I could have lightened my load.

The following recipes will hopefully inspire you to ask yourself, "Do I really need to throw that away?" I'd like to think that if you get anything from this cookbook, it is inspiration to use ingredients in the kitchen that you may not have used in the past.

The inspiration of my frugalness in the kitchen comes from my grandmother, who grew up during the Depression in a family of eleven. Can you imagine that?

Ironically, food is actually scarce around the world in various regions. Just because we aren't hungry today doesn't mean that hundreds of people out of our view aren't actually starving right now. I want to shed light on this, as chefs have for centuries. Most all of the best inventions in the kitchen have come from poor, underprivileged people who were creative and smart enough to find an answer to their cravings.

MIREPOIX *and* STOCK

Classically speaking, mirepoix is just a mixture of 50 percent onions, 25 percent celery and 25 percent carrots. The mirepoix of the South is known as the "Holy Trinity" and it consists of 50 percent onions, 25 percent bell peppers and 25 percent celery. Note that you will need 3 pounds (1.4 kg) of mirepoix for every 10 pounds (4.6 kg) of bones. You can decide which type of bones—beef, chicken or pork—you will make your stock out of. Stock is a collagen-rich broth that adds body to sauces and dishes.

MAKES 8 TO 10 CUPS (1.8 TO 2.4 L)

MIREPOIX

2 large white onions, cut into quarters, skins and roots removed

1 bunch celery, cut into 3-inch (7.6-cm) pieces, root trimmed

1 bunch large carrots, cut into 3-inch (7.6-cm) pieces, unpeeled

STOCK

10 lb (4.6 kg) bones (beef femur bones, chicken backs or wings, or pork necks or ribs)

½ cup (113 g) tomato paste

While in the kitchen, if I have any variety of these mirepoix veggies left over, I will toss them in a bag in the freezer until I can find the time to make stock. I will use scallions, shallots, stems of herbs—now that I think of it, I pretty much use everything.

Combine the onions, celery and carrots with the bones in a large hotel pan or large casserole dish, at least 12-inches (31-cm) long and cover the ingredients completely with cold water. The cold water allows for a stronger pull of the collagen within the bones. Hot water causes the collagen to tense up and it becomes more difficult to extract the very essence we are after. Stock should also never boil. It's best to cook it slow-and-low overnight in the oven at about 250°F (121°C).

Carefully remove the hotel pan from the oven and allow the stock to cool. Start to remove the bones from the stock and set them aside. Next, you can remove the cooked veggies. I usually just strain them out of the stock. This will make the stock easier to put into containers and store for use down the road.

Once you remove the bones from the oven, you can save them to make a second weaker stock of you wish. I like to store stock frozen in ice cube trays with different herbal infusions. Once the stock is poured into an ice cube tray, I will let a batch become frozen solid so then I can pop them into plastic bags, where they can last for weeks. The process of making stock is definitely worth it in the long run.

Paint the bones, backs, necks or ribs with the tomato paste. This acidic ingredient helps develop color and also helps extract the precious silky collagen.

In a deep, full-size hotel pan, roast your bones at 400°F (204°C) with 3 pounds (1.4 kg) mirepoix until a nice golden-brown color develops on the tomato paste. This will take about 20 minutes.

BEEF JERKY

There's something super addictive about chewing on salty pieces of tough meat. When meat is super tough and lean, it can be difficult to figure out what to do with those types of cuts. Cultures began creating various styles of jerky using pieces of the animal that were hard to eat.

You'll be pleasantly surprised at the various types of jerky you can make at home without a dehydrator. They didn't have dehydrators back in the good ol' days, but they were able to create or find heat sources to dry their meat out. This recipe is intended for beginners who don't have a food dehydrator.

MAKES 1 ½ LB (680 G)

4 tbsp (30 g) smoked paprika

2 tbsp (15 g) dry mustard

2 tbsp (15 g) cracked black pepper

1 tbsp (15 g) salt

½ cup (120 ml) soy sauce

½ cup (120 ml) Worcestershire sauce

1 tbsp (14 g) packed brown sugar

1 tbsp (15 ml) bourbon

3 lb (1.4 kg) sliced round or knuckle, cut with the grain ¼-inch (6-mm) thick (if it appears a little thick, you can take the flat side of a cleaver and smooth it out to your desired thickness)

Preheat the oven to 200°F (93°C).

Mix the smoked paprika, dry mustard, black pepper and salt for a dry rub in a small bowl. Place meat slices in the rub, coating both sides. Shake off excess.

In a clean, never-used squirt bottle, combine the soy sauce, Worcestershire sauce, brown sugar and bourbon. Lay out the thin slices of meat on 2 sheet trays and spray them with the curing mixture before putting the sheet trays in the oven.

I like to come back every 30 minutes and give the meat another coating of jerky essence. After 3 hours of heat, the jerky should be done. You can tell it's ready by how much it has shrunk. You will also notice a change in taste and texture as it becomes both chewy and salty.

This jerky makes a great snack and salad topper. It is perfect for road trips and also makes an awesome gift. I store my jerky in plastic bags and keep it in the fridge until I'm packing for the day. The jerky lasts for a few weeks this way.

Slicing the meat as thinly as possible, ¼ inch (6 mm) is fine. It helps to freeze the meat partially before slicing.

Place slices of meat onto sheet trays after being baptized in the dry rub.

Fill the entire tray so that the pieces of meat are barely touching.

GRINDS

When you start cutting more and more of your own meat at home, you will notice that there are quite a few meat scraps left over. In the past, you probably threw them in the trash.

Now, it's time to start saving them and using them just like a butcher shop does!

There are a ton of fun things to do with grinds. You make your own burgers and sausages, for starters. You can play around with different types of fat ratios and grind sizes too.

More often than not, I am too busy in the kitchen to drop what I'm doing to grind some meat that I've just trimmed. So what I do is set myself up for success. Here are the principles I follow:

Proper temperature: When working with meat, it's important to keep it cold. It's our responsibility in the kitchen to work clean so we can ensure our guests that no one will get sick. While I trim meat, I like to keep it in a plastic container with a lid next to me so I can quickly store it in the refrigerator in between tasks.

Proper storage: Best case scenario, all you'd ever have left over from cutting meat are tender fibers, riddled with fat. That's rarely ever the case, though. Generally, you will have three different types of by-products that you can use in different ways. They should be separated and used accordingly. One of the best investments you'll ever make is buying a roll of butcher's paper. It's the best way to store this stuff. I love having tons of little labeled packages in my freezer to play with.

Pure muscle (beef, veal, pork, chicken, bison, etc.): Cut the muscle into 1-inch (2.5-cm) chunks or smaller, depending on the type of grinder you have at home. Make sure silver skin is removed. You can most definitely toss the silver skin. It's inedible and will clog up your grinders. Period.

Fat: Fat is flavor. I can't stress that enough. Different types of fats have different flavor profiles and will therefore have different effects on your dishes. I separate my fats from my proteins so I can custom blend them for various dishes I'm making. Fat is also great for seasoning equipment, like your favorite cast iron pan. For example, I save all the residual bacon fat when I cook bacon. It's great to cook apples or bake with.

Bones and other collagen-like materials: If you can't grind it, then you can make a stock with it. These collagen-rich bones and similar tissues pretty much just make meat gelatin. Who knew bones could be so delicious?

When making any kind of meat grinds that are infused with seasonings, always cook a small piece of the mix off before cooking with the whole batch. This little "tester" piece serves a valuable purpose. Just sear a cute-size piece up in a pan for a minute on each side, until done. You might find after sampling your wares that you have, in fact, made the best sausage in the world, or that it needs a little something. So you better write that down! If the latter has occurred, this gives you the chance to fix the situation by adjusting the seasonings in your custom meat grind.

At the end of the day, if you're not down for the whole meat grinding experience, that's fine. I know a place where you can get some freshly ground pork, beef and veal. It's called a butcher shop. You can at least season your own Italian sausage grinds, right? If that seems like it's too much for you at the time, no biggie—the people behind the counter will know just what to do. I used to make custom sausages for my clients at the butcher shop all the time. Some wouldn't like flavors of sage or didn't want any spiciness in the Italian sausage. Where else would you get such a customizable experience? A real butcher shop.

Chapter 6

LET THE SEASONS MAKE THE SIDES:

～ Accompaniments That Reflect Yearly Changes ～

I get asked all the time, "What's your favorite thing to cook?" I struggled for a few years with what to say to a question like that. So many dishes would come to mind. The only definitive thing I could think of has become an answer that garnishes a lot of respect, while paying tribute to the farmers who make all my dishes possible. My answer is this, "It depends on where I'm at in the world, and what time of year it is." How much more simple could it get than that? Simplicity is the muse of the following recipes. I invite you to go out to the farmers' market and let the ingredients talk to you. Pick them up, smell them, ask questions. Be adventurous. Make mistakes and learn from them. That's what cooking real food is all about.

As a cook, you're only as good as the ingredients you're able to come across. You can't make a very good tomato sauce from tomatoes that aren't juicy and red, or don't smell like tomatoes. I'm inviting you to really take an honest look at the ingredients you're buying. Go big or go home. We only get one body so we might as well cherish it. Get organic if you can, and talk to the local farmers—they are a great resource for knowledge into what's in season now and what will be. Go out there and get your hands dirty.

SOUTHERN-STYLE SHRIMP COCKTAIL

This awesome mescal-infused cocktail is just what the party ordered. It's like a Bloody Mary that went to Mardi Gras.
You can pick whatever size of shrimp you want—it's all about how much work you want to put into it. Cooked, uncooked, peeled,
deveined . . . At the end of the day, you want to have cooked shrimp that is unshelled, deveined and tailless. If I'm in a hurry,
I'll just buy a bag of cooked and cleaned shrimp with the tail on. It's pretty easy to rip the tail off a few shrimp.

SERVES 8

1 lb (455 g) shrimp

8 cups (1.9 L) tomato juice

1 (12-oz [340-g]) can chipotle peppers, diced, sauce reserved

½ cup (120 ml) Worcestershire sauce

½ cup (120) freshly squeezed lemon or lime juice

1 bunch fresh cilantro, finely chopped, no stems

16 oz (480 ml) mescal

Salt and freshly cracked black pepper, to taste

Mix the shrimp, tomato juice, chipotle peppers and reserved sauce, Worcestershire sauce, lemon juice, cilantro, mescal and salt and pepper together in a large bowl and refrigerate until guests arrive. Serve Southern-Style Shrimp Cocktail in a small drink glass with a fork.

CORN, TOMATO *and* SMOKY BLUE CHEESE SALAD

There's nothing like corn on the cob. I love to fire up the grill and enjoy summer's wares. Smoked blue cheese really highlights the taste of the grill as well as the tomatoes. This is a crowd pleaser.

SERVES 4

4 fresh ears corn, husk removed and smeared with 3 tbsp (42 g) soft butter

2 large tomatoes, sliced into thick rounds

Salt and freshly cracked black pepper, to taste

4 oz (92 g) smoked blue cheese

1 bunch finely chopped fresh parsley

Cook the corn on the grill until it starts to become golden brown on all sides. Once it's done cooking, place the ears of corn on a few thick slices of tomato.

Season the tomato with the salt and pepper and sprinkle the corn and tomato with the smoked blue cheese and chopped parsley.

OYSTERS ROCKEFELLER *with* CELERY MIGNONETTE

I remember the first time I ate oysters prepared this way. They are one of my favorite dishes of all time. I have changed the lives of several people who at one time thought they didn't like oysters. Once they tried this recipe, their love affair with oysters finally began. The celery mignonette is a bright, acidic sauce that makes any seafood come to life. The bits of celery bring the refreshing crunch to the max.

SERVES 2

CELERY MIGNONETTE

½ shallot, small dice

1 tbsp (13 g) diced celery

3 tbsp (45 ml) red wine vinegar

1 tsp Dijon mustard

1 tsp packed brown sugar

1 dozen fresh oysters, on the half shell

4 oz (113 g) bacon, cut into ¼-inch (6-mm) pieces

3 cloves garlic, slivered

1 shallot, small dice

2 lemons, juiced and zested

1 cup (240 ml) white wine

2 handfuls (about ½ lb [227 g]) fresh spinach

2 cups (241 g) breadcrumbs (the ones made with old bread from home are best)

6 oz (170 g) grated Parmesan cheese

Create the mignonette first. Dice the shallot and celery before combining in a small bowl with the vinegar, mustard and brown sugar. It can be stored in the fridge for up to 2 weeks.

When storing fresh oysters in the fridge, do so uncovered and on ice. Oysters are living, breathing things. If you spot an oyster that is open, it's dead and isn't safe to eat.

The hard part's getting into the oysters. You can use a paint can opener or a flat-head screwdriver if you don't have an actual oyster shucker to unhinge one shell from the other. I like to nestle the whole oyster between a thick cloth towel so that I can get some leverage. The towel also protects me from hurting my hands. Clean the shell shrapnel from the raw oyster and remove it from its little foot that attaches it to its shell. This is nice because it makes enjoying them much easier once they are broiled.

To make the filling, mix together the bacon, garlic and shallot in a pan over medium-high heat until golden brown. Add the lemon juice, zest and white wine to the mix and reduce by half. Turn off the heat and add the spinach and breadcrumbs.

Turn the oven on to broil. Immediately fill the oysters with the filling and grate fresh cheese right on top of the oysters. Put the oysters directly under the flame until the cheese is melted and has developed a nice amount of color.

Serve the oysters immediately, with a drizzle of the mignonette. These do not make good leftovers, but the filling can be made ahead of time.

Butcher Babe Tip

I like to use fresh bread that has been cut into small pieces and toasted in the oven for breadcrumbs. Take your bread cubes and toast at 300°F (149°C) for about 15 minutes, or until softly golden brown. If you don't want to mess with all that, you can just buy some unseasoned breadcrumbs.

PANZANELLA SALAD SKEWERS

Who doesn't love big and crunchy croutons on a salad? I'm talking about freshly toasted and drenched in olive oil type of croutons you find on a panzanella salad. That salad is kind of boring though; it's only composed of tomatoes, basil and olive oil. One additional thing about salads is that most are difficult to eat (at least gracefully) at gatherings with friends and parties. With this fact being true, I took the challenge upon myself to make a quick party bite for even the most health-conscious of guests. Spicy pepperoni, roasted eggplant, creamy mozzarella and fresh basil will leave you saying, "What's not to love?" I combined all the flavors of my favorite antipasto salad fixin's and introduced them to the freshly toasted bread of the panzanella salad, bringing them together to form the unforgettable flavors of the Panzanella Salad Skewer. We've got a ton of flavor just on one stick.

MAKES 6 SKEWERS

1 small eggplant, peeled

2 large red bell peppers, seeds removed and cut into 12 square pieces

1 small (12-oz [340-g]) jar pickled whole pepperoncini peppers

1 (8-oz [227-g]) container small mozzarella balls

1 pint (473-ml) package small cherry tomatoes

½-lb (228-g) tube pepperoni, cut into ¼-inch (6-mm) wedges

1 small loaf ciabatta or focaccia bread, cut into 1-inch (2.5-cm) pieces

Olive oil, to taste

Balsamic vinegar, to taste

Fresh Parmesan cheese, for garnish

1 bunch fresh basil, for garnish

Preheat the oven to 350°F (177°C). Soak skewers in water for at least 15 minutes. Cut all the ingredients into squares or cubes that are roughly the same size to promote even cooking and start layering them onto the skewers in random order. This is also a fun interactive dish to set up for a party where guests can create a custom skewer of their own.

Once the skewers are complete, place them on a sheet tray and drizzle them with the olive oil and bake them for 10 to 12 minutes. When they come out of the oven, drizzle them with the balsamic vinegar. Garnish them with grated Parmesan cheese and some fresh basil leaves and you're done!

CORNDOG CASSEROLE

This side dish tastes like the state fair. 'Cuz who hasn't enjoyed a crispy corndog while gazing up at a Ferris wheel? Too bad you can't get corndogs at more places throughout the year. Well, now you can. It's a lot healthier and easier to make since you don't have to fire up the fryer. I love this dish, especially with some ketchup.

SERVES 4

1 (8½-oz [241-g]) box cornbread mix

1 (14-oz [397-g]) can cream corn

1 egg

½ cup (120 ml) milk

¼ cup (38 g) diced celery

1 tbsp (15 ml) vegetable oil

8 nitrate-free hot dogs cut into thin pieces on the bias, or 10 oz (283 g) smoked andouille sausage

Preheat the oven to 350°F (177°C).

In a small casserole dish, mix together the cornbread mix, cream corn, egg, milk and celery.

Heat a saucepan and add the vegetable oil. Toss the hot dogs into the pan and let them get nice and crispy. Add them to the top of the cornbread mixture and bake for 20 minutes or until the casserole is set in the center. Serve hot. Stays fresh in the fridge for up to 5 days. Reheat in the oven at 350°F (177°C) for 15 minutes. Serve with your favorite ketchup or mustard.

CRUSTACEAN CORN CAKES
and LEMON-SCALLION CREAM

What on Earth could be crispy, creamy, sweet and salty all at once? It's a Crustacean Corn Cake! These quick and simple bites can satiate the crabbiest of guests. This recipe is an upscale version of my Grandma Susie's creamy cornbread with the addition of real crabmeat. I haven't met one person who hasn't fallen in love with this concoction.

SERVES 8

1 (14-oz [397-g]) can cream corn

2 eggs

1 cup (180 g) shredded Parmigiano-Reggiano, divided

1 red bell pepper, small dice

1 cup (75 g) jumbo lump crabmeat, drained

1 (8½-oz [241-g]) box corn muffin mix

1 tsp smoked paprika

LEMON-SCALLION CREAM

1 cup (121 g) sour cream

Zest of 1 lemon

Juice of 1 lemon

1 bunch scallions

Freshly cracked black pepper and sea salt, to taste

Preheat the oven to 325°F (163°C). Combine the cream corn, eggs, ¾ cup (135 g) of the Parmigiano-Reggiano, bell pepper and crabmeat with a fork in a medium bowl. Add the corn muffin mix to the cream corn mixture until it's barely combined. For 8 single servings, line a muffin pan with paper liners and fill them three-quarters of the way full. If you don't have a scoop, you can use 2 large spoons instead. Sprinkle the corn cakes with the remaining ¼ cup (45 g) Parmigiano-Reggiano and smoked paprika. Bake until golden brown and the centers are nearly set, about 15 to 17 minutes.

While the corn cakes are baking, make the lemon-scallion cream.

Put the sour cream in a small bowl and add the lemon zest and lemon juice. Finely chop the green tops of the scallions and add them to the bowl with the other ingredients. Season the lemon-scallion cream with the salt and pepper.

SPICY SWINE MUSHROOM CAPS

Mushrooms have amazing flavor profiles. There are so many different kinds and textures. I love using portabella mushrooms because they are like bowls begging to be filled with something delicious! In this case, we stuff the baby portabella mushrooms with a homemade spicy pork sausage infused with cheese. These make great appetizers and as a topper for baked potatoes. Mmmmmm cheese.

MAKES 12-18 MUSHROOM CAPS

24 oz (680 g) baby portabella mushrooms or 4 large portabella mushroom caps

2 tbsp (30 ml) olive oil

SPICY SWINE GRIND

1½ lb (683 g) ground pork

1 tbsp (3 g) fresh thyme leaves

1 tsp red chili flakes

1 tsp smoked paprika, plus more as needed

2 tsp (6 g) caraway seeds

1 tbsp (3 g) fresh oregano leaves, chopped

1 tbsp (3 g) fresh sage leaves, chopped

¼ cup (60 ml) red wine

1 tbsp (15 g) salt

1 tbsp (15 g) freshly cracked black pepper

1 egg

6 oz (170 g) Havarti cheese (or any creamy melting cheese), shredded

Preheat the oven to 350°F (177°C).

Pop off the mushroom stems and save them for the filling. Remove the gills from the inside of the mushroom caps with a small spoon by gently scraping the brown flakes out of the mushrooms. Be careful not to tear away any of the mushroom caps. Discard the gills. Rinse the stems and freshly cleaned caps under cool running water. Pat them dry with a paper towel.

Grease a baking dish with the olive oil. Set the mushrooms side-by-side in the baking dish.

In a medium bowl, mix the fresh ground pork with the thyme, red chili flakes, smoked paprika, caraway seeds, oregano, sage, red wine, salt, pepper, egg and Havarti until combined.

Divide the raw pork filling among the mushroom caps with heaping spoonfuls. Dust the tops with additional smoked paprika for extra color and flavor.

Bake the mushroom caps for 20 minutes or until golden brown. Serve hot. If you choose to save and reheat the mushroom caps, do so in a 350°F (177°C) oven for 15 minutes.

Place the mushrooms bottoms-up on a baking dish, gills removed.

Fill the mushrooms with a heaping amount of filling and place in a preheated oven.

You better make sure these are good before you serve 'em! Careful, they are hot!

BOUDIN BALLS *with* BOURBON MUSTARD

I remember eating boudin on a saltine cracker with hot sauce as a little girl like it was yesterday. I was at a little truck stop in Baton Rouge when I had this local comfort food for the first time. While boudin is one of my favorite Louisiana comfort foods, making it can be a pretty long, labor-intensive process. This quicker version allows you to get a similar result without all the fuss of grinding the meat, casing it and having to wait a few hours to eat it!

MAKES 18 (2-OUNCE [57-G]) BALLS

4 cups (960 ml) water

1 small white onion

5 cloves garlic

1 green bell pepper

½ heart celery

2 tsp (10 g) cayenne pepper

1 tbsp (15 g) salt

1 tbsp (15 g) freshly cracked black pepper

1½ lb (683 g) ground pork butt (the fattier, the better)

½ lb (228 g) pork liver, ground (if you choose to not use pork liver, substitute more pork butt)

3 cups (483 g) cooked medium-grain rice

1 bunch scallions, cut into thin pieces

1 bunch parsley, finely chopped

8 oz (228 g) dried breadcrumbs

BOURBON MUSTARD

¼ cup (60 ml) bourbon

2 tbsp (28 g) packed brown sugar

1 shallot, small dice

½ cup (118 ml) Dijon mustard

¼ cup (60 ml) Louisiana-style hot sauce

Pulse the water, onion, garlic, bell pepper, celery, cayenne pepper, salt and pepper in a food processor until chunky.

In a heavy-bottomed saucepan, combine the ground pork butt and liver with the processed vegetables.

Simmer for 30 minutes over medium heat while breaking up chunks of cooked pork. When the mixture is done cooking, chill it in the refrigerator for 2 hours or until completely cold. You may have to crumble the cooked pork a bit more.

Add the cooked rice, scallions and parsley. Mix until combined.

Preheat the oven to 400°F (204°C). With a 2-ounce (57-g) scoop, portion the boudin mix into well-compacted balls. Roll the balls in the breadcrumbs until coated and place them in an oven-safe dish. You can also bake this mixture like a casserole if you like.

To make the bourbon mustard, combine the bourbon, brown sugar and shallot in a small saucepan over high heat for about 5 minutes or until the bourbon cooks out. Remove the mixture from the heat and add the Dijon mustard and hot sauce. Mix thoroughly. Store the bourbon mustard in the refrigerator. It stays fresh for 30 days.

Arrange the boudin balls so that they are not touching in the dish. Bake for 25 minutes. When the balls are done, remove them from the oven and serve immediately with the bourbon mustard. Reheat the boudin balls in the oven at 350°F (177°C) until an internal temperature of 150°F (66°C) is achieved.

LARDON AUX ARUGULA SALAD

The colder months of the year aren't exactly known for their salads. This is the type of salad you eat in the colder months.
You feel good about it because the word "salad" is in its name, but it also has hearty bacon in it.
It's a great dish for anytime of the day, even breakfast. I'll take two of 'em!

SERVES 4

4 oz (113 g) thick-cut or slab bacon, cut into ½-inch (13-mm) pieces

¼ lb (113 g) haricot verts or green beans, cut into thirds, tips removed

1 shallot, thinly sliced

½ tbsp (7 ml) Dijon mustard

3 tbsp (45 ml) red wine vinegar

1 (5-oz [142-g]) package arugula

4 oz (113 g) Gruyère cheese

1 tsp salt

1 tsp freshly cracked black pepper

POACHED EGGS

4 cups (960 ml) water

3 tbsp (45 ml) distilled white vinegar

4 eggs

In a saucepan over medium-low heat, begin to render the fat from the pieces of bacon. The process of rendering the bacon fat takes about 15 minutes. When the bacon is good and crispy, add the haricot verts, shallot, Dijon mustard and red wine vinegar and continue to cook for about 5 minutes. Remove the pan from the heat and set aside.

Time to poach the eggs to top this glorious salad! In a small saucepan, combine the water and white vinegar. Bring the water to a boil. I add my eggs one at a time. Poaching eggs can be tricky. Right before you add the egg to the boiling water, remove the saucepan from the heat for a moment, so that the egg can be dropped into less "choppy" waters. As soon as the egg exits the shell and is submerged in the poaching liquid, return the saucepan to the heat. A soft poached egg takes about 1½ minutes while a hard poached egg takes about 3 minutes. Be careful when you remove the egg from the water with a slotted spoon. I lay my eggs on a paper towel to soak up the residual water before placing them on top of the salad. As soon as all your eggs finish poaching, start plating the salad.

Place the arugula in a mixing bowl and pour the bacon mixture on top of it. Toss the salad so the ingredients are all incorporated. Divide the salad mixture between 4 plates. Carefully place a poached egg on top of each salad. Garnish with the Gruyère, salt and pepper. Serve immediately.

BACON 'N' TATER CHOWDER

Anyone can make this soup. It's quick and easy. After a long day, nothing hits the spot like this does. It doesn't take very many ingredients, either, which is a good thing because you can't get all those fresh, farm-raised veggies during the fall. So it's only natural we resort back to the good ol' standby known as meat and potatoes.

SERVES 6-8

1 lb (455 g) bacon, cut into ½-inch (13-mm) strips

4 tbsp (56 g) butter, divided

3 dried bay leaves

1 tbsp (15 g) salt, plus more to taste

1 tbsp (15 g) freshly cracked black pepper, plus more to taste

4 medium Idaho potatoes, cut into ½-inch (13-mm) cubes, peeled or unpeeled

1 white onion, small dice

1 celery heart, small dice

½ cup (125 g) all-purpose flour

8 cups (1.9 L) chicken stock

8 cups (1.9 L) milk

1 (4-oz [113-g]) package instant potatoes

1 bunch scallions, sliced

1 (8-oz [228-g]) package shredded sharp cheddar cheese (Havarti, Parmesan and Colby Jack all work well too)

Add the bacon, butter, bay leaves, salt and pepper to a heavy-bottomed, 6-quart (5.8-L) stockpot over medium-low heat. Cook this mixture on the stovetop for 15 minutes. Cooking it on a lower heat allows for the fat from the bacon to render.

Add 1 tablespoon (15 g) of butter to a Dutch oven and sauté the potatoes, onion and celery on the stovetop until slightly browned.

After the bacon has become browned slightly, sprinkle in the flour to start making a roux. I use a wooden spoon to combine the fat and flour. Continue to cook the roux over medium heat for 5 minutes. Add the potato, onion and celery mixture.

Slowly start to pour in the chicken stock so that it becomes incorporated with the roux. The slower you add the liquid, the less chance you have of lumps developing in your chowder. Use a wooden spoon so you can mash out the bits of flour.

Once all the chicken stock is added, add the milk and instant potatoes. Keep the chowder on medium heat so that it won't boil, which will result in curdling the milk. Season the chowder with salt and additional pepper. Garnish the chowder with fresh scallions and shredded cheese on top. Serve hot. Reheat leftovers on the stovetop. If the chowder has become too thick, just add 1 cup (240 ml) of water.

SHRIMP *and* CORN CASSEROLE

Several times throughout my career, I have "accidentally on purpose" created some unforgettable dishes. More often than not,
I was just cleaning out the fridge and happened to make something delicious from what was hanging out in there.
This dish is an example of this phenomenon, resulting in a sweet and salty corn-infused casserole.
Its creamy texture melts into pieces of sweet whole shrimp tails.

SERVES 4

1 (8½-oz [240-g]) box cornbread mix

4 cups (960 ml) chicken stock

2 cups (480 ml) milk

6 eggs

¼ cup (38 g) cornstarch

1 tbsp (15 g) salt

1 tsp freshly cracked black pepper

2 lb (910 g) fresh or frozen corn
(not canned corn)

1 bunch parsley, roughly chopped

6 cloves garlic, minced

12 raw shrimp (shell off, deveined, no tail)

8 oz (228 g) Parmesan cheese

Preheat the oven to 300°F (149°C). In a large mixing bowl, combine the cornbread mix, chicken stock, milk, eggs, cornstarch, salt and pepper until smooth. Next, add the corn, parsley and garlic.

Pour this mixture into a large casserole dish, allowing a ½ inch (13 mm) of space from the top of the pan. Cover the dish with foil and bake for 45 minutes. Remove the foil and place the shrimp on the top of the nearly set casserole.

Turn the oven up to 375°F (191°C). Top the casserole with the Parmesan and bake for an additional 15 minutes. Remove the casserole from the oven and allow it to cool for 10 minutes while the dish sets up. Serve hot. This casserole makes great leftovers. Reheat them in the oven at 350°F (177°C) for 20 minutes.

CHICKEN VOODOO SOUP

As a little girl growing up in Louisiana, I was no stranger to big and bold spicy flavors. My dad was always in the kitchen concocting some elaborate bizarre Cajun-themed dish that would almost leave my mouth on fire. One time in particular, I happened to not be feeling well and he took it upon himself to chef up something that would magically turn my health around. To my surprise the "voodoo" he created in the kitchen that day never left my palate's memory. Essentially, this is the hot and sour soup of Louisiana. Its tangy broth will leave you wondering if there is something magical in that pot.

SERVES 8

2 tbsp (30 ml) vegetable oil

4 bone-in, skin-on chicken breasts (2 to 3 lb [910 g to 1.6 kg] total)

1 tbsp (15 g) salt

1 tbsp (15 g) black pepper

12 oz (340 g) andouille sausage links, cut into ½-inch (13-mm) pieces

1 celery heart, medium dice

1 red bell pepper, medium dice, seeds removed

2 sweet white onions, medium dice

4 large carrots, peeled and roughly chopped

6 to 8 cloves garlic, crushed

3 dried bay leaves

2 tbsp (14 g) smoked paprika

1 (14-oz [397-g]) can fire-roasted tomatoes

1 (15-oz [425-ml]) bottle Worcestershire sauce

½ cup (120 ml) red wine vinegar

1 (4-qt [4-L]) box chicken stock

1 cup (144 g) long-grain wild rice

Cayenne pepper, to taste

1 bunch fresh parsley, roughly chopped

A few handfuls (½ lb [227 g]) fresh spinach

Freshly squeezed lemon juice, to taste

Pour the vegetable oil into a 6-quart (5.8-L) stockpot. Turn your stovetop burner on medium-low heat. Season the chicken breasts with the salt and pepper. Gently lay the seasoned chicken skin-side down in the stockpot.

Now that the chicken is searing, go ahead and toss in the andouille sausage. Cover the pan with a lid. Let the chicken skin slowly render in its delicious, golden fat along with the andouille. This should take about 15 to 20 minutes, or until the internal temperature at the thickest point of the chicken breasts reads 150°F (66°C).

Remove the lid of the stockpot. Toss the celery, bell pepper, onions, carrots, garlic, bay leaves and smoked paprika right on top of the chicken and andouille. Add the fire-roasted tomatoes, Worcestershire sauce, red wine vinegar and chicken stock and stir to combine. The tangy acidity of these liquids allows you to easily remove the delicious golden-brown pan drippings and the chicken breasts. Place the whole breasts in the refrigerator to cool. When they are completely cool, you will be able to shred them with ease. What do you do with the skin? Eat it. (I won't tell anyone.)

To thicken up this delicious soup, just toss the rice into the simmering pot. Slow-and-low is the key here. Place the lid back on and allow 30 to 40 minutes for the rice to cook completely. The rice will puff up and burst as an indication it's done cooking. This natural occurrence adds the body and thickness you want to find in a hearty soup. Right before serving, add the chilled shredded chicken. Add the cayenne pepper, parsley, spinach and lemon juice.

Butcher Babe Tips

* Always buy bone-in, skin-on chicken. Why? It costs less. The reduced amount of fabrication means that a meat cutter didn't have to spend as much time breaking down the product. Time is money. The bones are naturally rich in collagen (I like to call it "bone butter"), which adds that coveted luscious mouthfeel. As for chicken skin, it's just delicious and when finessed properly, it's mouthwatering. Pat the skin dry, season with salt and slowly sear for perfect a golden brown every time.

* The chicken breasts will continue to cook even after being removed from their heat source. This scientific phenomenon is known as carry-over cooking. Let the thermometer act as a magic wand defending you and your loved ones from eating dried out chicken. You are officially on your way to becoming a full-fledged kitchen magician!

OYSTER STUFFING

Every winter holiday, my grandma makes Oyster Stuffing. I look forward to it in particular more than any other side dish she makes. It's crispy and buttery, and it sticks to your ribs. Did I mention it's got oysters in it? Oh boy, do I love oysters.

SERVES 8

1 large loaf pre-sliced rye bread

1 lb (455 g) oysters in liquor (oysters that have been removed from the shell and are submerged in an oyster-infused liquid called oyster liquor), oyster liquor reserved

4 tbsp (56 g) butter

1 white onion, small dice

1 celery heart, small dice

2 tsp (2 g) fresh sage

1 tsp fresh rosemary

1 tsp salt

1 tsp freshly cracked black pepper

1 bunch fresh parsley, roughly chopped

6 eggs

6 cups (1.4 L) chicken stock

Preheat the oven to 350°F (177°C). Cut the loaf of rye bread into 1-inch (2.5-cm) cubes and place them on a baking sheet. Toast the bread cubes for 15 minutes in the oven. Set aside to cool.

Remove the oysters from the liquor and place them in a bowl. Reserve liquor for the liquid portion of the recipe. (Never throw oyster liquor away—it's meant to be cooked with.) Leave the oysters under refrigeration until you are ready to top off the stuffing with them.

In a large cast iron pan over medium heat, melt the butter and sweat the onion, celery, sage, rosemary, salt, pepper and parsley until the onions are clear. Remove the pan from the stovetop and place it into the hot oven. Place the toasted bread cubes back into a large mixing bowl and start to combine them with the cooked onion mixture.

In a large bowl, whisk the eggs, chicken stock and reserved oyster liquor until combined. Pour the liquid mixture into the mixing bowl with the bread cubes, agitating them so that all the pieces are soaked with the liquid.

After about 15 minutes of soaking, carefully pour the stuffing mix into the cast iron pan. The hot cast iron makes for a nice and crispy stuffing! Pat down the stuffing so that it's evenly distributed. Take the oysters from the fridge and randomly place them on top of the stuffing. Bake the stuffing for 35 minutes or until golden brown. Serve hot.

ALASKAN SALMON BUNDLES

These little creamy bites of heaven are reminiscent of the lox bagel that we all know and love. These bundles are designed for a nice relaxing brunch at home, when you're curled up on the couch with the ones you love.

SERVES 4

1 (14¾-oz [418-g]) can salmon, drained and meat broken into smaller pieces

2 (3-oz [85-g]) packages cream cheese, softened

½ cup (25 g) sliced scallions

4 tsp (20 ml) freshly squeezed lemon juice

1 tsp fresh dill

1 (8-oz [227-g]) package crescent rolls

Preheat the oven to 350°F (177°C).

In a small bowl, combine the salmon, cream cheese, scallions, lemon juice and dill. Unroll the crescent dough and separate it into 8 rectangles. On each rectangle, press the center diagonal seam together to make a solid crust.

Spoon ¼ cup (55 g) of the salmon filling near a short side of the rectangle. Fold over the short side of the dough so the edges meet. Close the edges with a fork to seal the salmon bundles. Place the bundles on a baking sheet and bake for 15 to 17 minutes, until golden brown and puffy. Serve warm.

BUTTERED FRENCH RADISHES

Down South, it's no secret that butter makes everything better. I grew up watching my grandma eat slices of radishes with butter on white bread thinking she was crazy. Years later, I realized what a French-inspired, classy little snack my grandma was chowing down on! This is an elevated version of that sandwich.

SERVES 4

1 large bunch pristine radishes (must have healthy green leaves)

8 oz (228 g) butter

1 tbsp (15 g) fancy salt, such as Maldon, smoked sea salt (something visually appealing)

1 tsp freshly cracked black pepper

1 tbsp (3 g) fresh dill

Picking out the right bunch of radishes is the most difficult part of this whole recipe. You are looking for those beautiful, healthy bunches of radishes with bold green leafy tops. The leafy tops, as you will discover, are pretty fragile. If I happen to accidentally separate the leafy greens from the radish, it's no big deal. I'll just have it as a little snack.

Gently wash the radishes under cool running water to remove any excess dirt. I like to use a paper towel also. With a paring knife, remove any not-so-beautiful leaves and discard them. Lay out the cleaned, pristine radishes on a few pieces of clean paper towel close to a cutting board. With a sharp knife, remove a minimal amount of radish near the root end. The goal is to create a smooth surface the radish can "sit" on.

In a small metal mixing bowl over low heat on the stovetop, gently melt the butter. I use a small whisk to bring the butter from completely cold to the perfect dipping texture. There shouldn't be any chunks of butter floating around. Once the butter has been tempered over the heat, gently place a radish into the butter while carefully holding its stems. Coat the radish about three-quarters of the way up. Shake off any excess butter and also swipe the bottom of the radish on the butter bowl.

Lightly sprinkle the radishes with salt, pepper and dill and place them in a serving dish. Serve immediately.

You may have some radishes that didn't have gloriously perfect tops. That's fine, clean 'em and make them into pickles.

Prepare the radishes for their butter baths by cutting the bottoms off so they may stand up on their own.

After giving them a dip, remove any excess butter on the sides of the bowl.

FRIED GREEN TOMATOES

In the South, fried green tomatoes are easy to find. Everyone's got their own special way they cook and eat them. The way I like to make mine is pretty straightforward. As long as you like fried vegetables, you'll be happy with this dish. If you haven't had fried green tomatoes before, the best comparison I can make is with a fried pickle chip. If you like that, then you'll love this.

SERVES 4

4 cups (960 ml) vegetable oil

Salt and freshly cracked black pepper, to taste

6 firm green tomatoes, cut into ½-inch (13-mm) thick slices

3 cups (750 g) all-purpose flour

½ cup (76 g) cornstarch

2 cups (480 ml) milk

4 eggs

2 lb (910 g) panko breadcrumbs

1 tbsp (7 g) smoked paprika

1 tsp freshly cracked black pepper

Fill a medium saucepan with the vegetable oil. Heat the oil to 350°F (177°C).

Salt and pepper both sides of the tomato slices. Place the flour and cornstarch in a pie tin or other shallow dish. In a second dish, whisk together the milk and eggs until smooth. In a third dish, mix together the panko breadcrumbs, smoked paprika and pepper.

Dredge the tomatoes in the first dish, then the second, then the third. I like to use a pair of chopsticks to move the tomatoes from one pan to the next so I don't have to get covered in flour.

Last but not least, gently put 2 pieces of dredged tomato in the hot oil at a time. They only take about 4 minutes to cook. Remove the tomatoes from the oil when they are done and place them on a paper towel. Serve hot.

ASPARAGUS TART

This tart goes great with everything. It could be breakfast, lunch or dinner. It's kind of like a quiche when it really comes down to it. Feel free to have fun creating a variety of different flavor profiles by switching up the cheese and veggie combinations. I love to make this tart and keep it in the fridge until I want a piece. It's super easy to cut and reheat in the oven. It's also great to bring to friends' houses because it travels so well.

MAKES 1 (9-INCH [23-CM]) TART

1 sheet puff pastry dough

1 cup (240 ml) milk

4 eggs

2 cups (260 g) grated Gruyère cheese, divided

1 tsp salt

1 tsp freshly cracked black pepper

¼ tsp ground nutmeg

1 bunch fresh asparagus, trimmed approximately 1 inch (2.5 cm) above the root end

1 scallion

Preheat the oven to 325°F (163°C).

Place the puff pastry dough inside a tart pan. Trim the excess dough.

In a medium mixing bowl, combine the milk, eggs, 1 cup (180 g) of the Gruyère, salt, pepper and nutmeg until the eggs are completely incorporated.

Cut asparagus and scallion on the bias into 1-inch (2.5-cm) pieces. Place them into the tart pan before you pour in the milk mixture. This method allows you to easily place the veggies where you want them in the pan. Otherwise, they will just float around in the milk mixture.

Place the tart pan in the oven with a sheet tray underneath it. Pour the milk mixture into the pan. The extra tray underneath acts like a barrier between the baking tart and the oven floor. More often than not, tarts like this will bubble over a bit, creating that beautiful golden crust we all know and love.

Finish the top of the tart with the remaining 1 cup (180 g) Gruyère and bake for about 30 minutes. Let the tart cool for 10 minutes before serving. When the tart is set in the middle, it's time to serve it. This tart is great hot or as a leftover for several days.

GRAVLAX SALMON

If the salmon you use for this recipe has previously been frozen, that's fine; but make sure it still isn't frozen when making the recipe. I recommend using salmon that is of the thicker variety, also known as center cuts. In other words, you don't want to use "tail pieces" if you can help it. If you walk up to the fish counter and there are 2 (8-ounce [228-g]) pieces of even thickness, go ahead and grab those. Last but not least, I like to use only wild-caught salmon. It's not full of artificial coloring agents.

MAKES 1 LB (455 G) SMOKED SALMON

CURING MIX

2 tbsp (15 g) sea salt

1 tbsp (7 g) smoked paprika

1 tbsp (14 g) packed brown sugar

½ bunch fresh dill

2 tbsp (30 ml) bourbon

1 lb (455 g) fresh, skin-on salmon filet, bones removed

Line a small container with plastic wrap. Use one piece of plastic wrap that will be large enough to completely encase the salmon pieces once you cover them in the curing mix.

In a separate small bowl, combine the salt, smoked paprika, brown sugar, dill and bourbon. Set aside.

Cut the piece of salmon in half, separating it into 2 equal pieces. Set both pieces skin-side down in the plastic-wrapped container. Pour the curing mix over both pieces. You will now put both pieces of salmon on top of one another, so that they are touching flesh-to-flesh. Tightly wrap up the salmon pieces in plastic wrap, so that they are airtight. If you need to wrap these pieces again so that no curing mix can leak out, go for it. Better safe than sorry. Weigh down the salmon with something that will evenly distribute weight, such as a heavy lid to a pot.

Place the newly cured salmon under refrigeration. Every 12 hours, flip the salmon so that the curing mix can equally permeate the opposite piece of salmon. In my experience with this recipe, it's best to let the salmon cure for 48 hours. The curing process begins to harden the salmon after curing more than 3 days. I also am not a big advocate of keeping it lying around in the fridge after that 3-day mark. It's best enjoyed within 24 hours after the curing process is complete. It's kind of like having sushi for leftovers. Don't let its perishability deter you from making this, though. It's fun and is a great conversation piece.

Before serving the gravlax, carefully remove the excess curing mix. A pastry brush works great for that. After the excess is removed, I like to pop the gravlax into the freezer for about 30 minutes. Slightly freezing the fish makes is easier to slice into thin pieces. Freezing meat before slicing works for all proteins.

BRUSSELS SALAD

This salad is crunchy and healthy. It reminds me of all the salads I wasn't eating all winter. You've got to start somewhere in order to get bikini ready. I guess I'll start here. If you like a tangy, creamy salad with a healthy vibe, this one's for you. It's got a nice punch of spicy horseradish with an undertone of roasted sesame seeds. It's great on a burger or with some fresh avocado. You can find all these ingredients year round, to boot.

SERVES 2

DRESSING

¼ cup (45 g) tahini

¼ cup (57 g) sour cream

Juice of 1 lemon

2 tbsp (30 ml) red wine vinegar

1 tbsp (15 g) fresh horseradish

Salt and freshly cracked black pepper, to taste

1 lb (455 g) fresh Brussels sprouts, cleaned and cut into thin pieces

1 small head red cabbage, cleaned and cut into thin strips

¼ cup (10 g) fresh parsley, roughly chopped

½ red onion, sliced into thin strips

Combine the tahini, sour cream, lemon juice, red wine vinegar, fresh horseradish and salt and pepper to create the dressing for this light and refreshing salad. Keep refrigerated.

Place the Brussels sprouts, cabbage, parsley and onion in a large mixing bowl. Toss the dressing with the salad and serve! Keep this salad refrigerated in a container up to 3 days.

SMOKED SALMON DEVILED EGGS

When I started working as a private chef, I realized a few things. On one hand, my clients enabled me to create edible art for a living; on the other hand, I had to create a variety of art for people who would actually want to buy it. Oh, the story of the tortured artist— or chef, rather—unfolds. The food had to make sense while being relatable. My whimsical, creative side yearned to never make the same dish twice while the more sensible side of me just wanted to pay my bills. I often felt torn. When I created this deviled egg recipe, I had a breakthrough that immediately stopped my feelings of conflict.

The trick in sparking a foodie's interest lies in marrying something new with something old. I took the flavor of a lox bagel and made it into a gorgeous little bite of smoky heaven. I can't think of anyone who has ever been like, "Nah, I don't want to eat that."

Now, if I could just figure out how to take all the calories out of all this stuff, I'd be a millionaire.

MAKES 24 DEVILED EGGS

1 dozen large eggs

½ tsp baking soda per 4 cups (960 ml) water

¼ cup (60 g) cream cheese, softened

1 tbsp (15 ml) red wine vinegar

Zest of 1 lemon

1 tsp salt

1 tsp freshly cracked black pepper

2 oz (57 g) smoked salmon or Gravlax Salmon (page 153)

1 scallion

½ bunch fresh dill

Put the eggs in a medium-size saucepan and cover them completely with water, leaving at least an inch (2.5 cm) of water above the eggs. Add the baking soda to the water. Place the pan on the stovetop and turn the burner on to high. Wait for the water to come to a rolling boil. Once the water is at a rolling boil, turn off the heat, remove the pan from the stovetop and set it in the sink. Pour cool running water over the eggs for 2 minutes.

Gently tap the cooled eggs on the side of the sink, making small cracks all over the eggs' surfaces. Peel back the shell with the addition of a gentle stream of cool water helping you remove it.

Next, let the peeled eggs cool slightly. They will be fine if they are at least at room temperature.

Set out the dish you want to serve your deviled eggs on. Dip a sharp paring knife in water every time before you cut an egg in half. The addition of this moisture on the blade acts as a lubricant, decreasing the knife's drag and the amount of torn cooked eggs.

Place the egg yolks into a sifter. Press the cooked yolks through the sifter with the bottom of a spoon. This will result in a nice, fluffy egg filling. I do mine right over the bowl I'm going to make the filling in. After you "sift" the yolks, add the cream cheese, red wine vinegar, lemon zest, salt and pepper. Mix the filling by hand until it is thoroughly combined. Season with additional salt and pepper to taste. (I hold back on the salt slightly to account for the saltiness of the salmon.) Cut thin slices of salmon and scallion and tear off perky pieces of fresh dill for garnish. Set the garnishes aside.

In order to fill the eggs with the filling, place the filling in a pastry bag with a star tip, use a plastic bag with a hole cut in it or do it the old-fashioned way with 2 kitchen spoons.

Either way, fill the eggs up! Last but not least, garnish the deviled eggs with the salmon, scallion and dill. Serve cold. These deviled eggs last for 1 day in the fridge with the Gravlax Salmon, or 3 days with the smoked salmon.

Chapter 7

BOURBON AND BAKING:
∽ Desserts ∽

When I make desserts, I am teleported to another time and place. When I'm in the kitchen with my apron on, I'm the little girl I was years ago standing on a kitchen chair in my grandma's kitchen so that I could learn right beside one of the greats. Even though I'm a "grown up" now, I still approach ingredients like butter and sugar with the same childlike wonder. I hope that never changes. The only difference now is the regular appearance of bourbon. The hustle, bustle and stress of the world melts off me like chocolate sauce trickling down the side of a cake. I am making edible art, and I consider myself beyond blessed to be able to do that for a living.

Making desserts is all about finding your happy place and sharing that feeling with another person. We should all count ourselves very lucky if we have a good friend and a fine bottle of bourbon to go along with it. Sometimes I believe we ought to eat dessert first. Life is short, so let's stay sweet, count our blessings and celebrate one another. When's the last time you took someone on a "cake date?"

PISTACHIO POUND CAKE *with* TIPSY STRAWBERRIES AND ROYAL ICING

My great great cousin Eileen has been wowing her guests since the 1950s with this sweet treat. The simplicity of its ingredients goes to show that they don't make things like they used to, including cakes. For over a decade, I've kept this one tucked away in my arsenal of showstopping desserts. The cake is as timeless as the woman who made it and both have been known to pair nicely with a snuffer of top-shelf bourbon. Its golden exterior hides a buttery wonderland of caloric rapture! Behold the power of Aunt Eileen's pistachio pound cake.

SERVES 8

½ lb (228 g) (2 sticks) softened butter, plus more for prepping the cake pan

3 cups (750 g) all-purpose flour, plus more for prepping the cake pan

3 cups (576 g) sugar

¼ tsp baking soda

6 large eggs

1 cup (228 g) sour cream

1 tsp vanilla, almond or lemon extract

Roasted pistachios

TIPSY STRAWBERRIES

1 lb (455 g) fresh strawberries, tops removed

¼ cup (60 ml) brandy or bourbon

ROYAL ICING

3 cups (390 g) powdered sugar

Juice of 2 lemons

1 egg white

Preheat the oven to 325°F (163°C).

Prepare a Bundt cake pan or tube pan by smearing the inside with butter. I have found that I like to use the wrappers from the butter to grease the pan instead of throwing them away. Then just toss a spoonful of flour in the pan and tap away, making sure it's distributed evenly. Now you know the ol' greased and floured trick.

Cream together the butter and sugar in the bowl of an electric or stand mixer. The batter is really thick and difficult to mix by hand. I use a whisk to "sift" dry ingredients into a large mixing bowl or sheet of parchment paper, then use a large spoon to transport it into the creamed mixture. Works like a charm.

Add 2 eggs at a time to the mixture, scraping the sides of the bowl to ensure that you are creating a silky homogenous mixture. This is also a good time to try the cake batter. Well, actually, when's a bad time to try it? You tell me.

Stir in the sour cream by hand along with the vanilla extract.

Bake the cake for 30 minutes. Lower the oven to 300°F (149°C) and continue baking for 45 minutes or until a toothpick inserted in the middle of the cake comes out clean.

Let the cake cool completely before trying to remove it from the pan.

Wash and rinse strawberries in cool water. Pat dry. Cut the strawberries in half and place them in a bowl. Pour the brandy over the strawberries. Let the strawberries sit for 30 minutes at room temperature before serving.

In a medium bowl, mix together the powdered sugar, lemon juice and egg white. Pour over the top of the pistachio pound cake. Sprinkle the top of the cake with the pistachios. Let the icing set for 30 minutes. Right before you serve the pound cake, garnish it with the tipsy strawberries. Yum.

Butcher Babe Tip

If you don't have any sour cream lying around, I've used various flavors of yogurt in this cake with great success and hope you'll try the same.

BOURBON BALLS *with* CANDIED PECANS

My dad used to make these when I was growing up. He would disappear into the kitchen for several hours while he made his holiday bourbon balls. He would reappear rosy cheeked, like a little Christmas elf excited to share his wares. I still can't figure out to this day how he got those little chocolate balls to taste so much like bourbon. They were the type of chocolatey bites someone might have to turn down because they had to drive home later that night. I love these things. They bring a fun memory to my heart and a warmth to my belly. Thanks, Dad.

MAKES 2 DOZEN, 1-OUNCE (928-G) BALLS

6 oz (171 ml) heavy whipping cream

1 tsp salt

4 oz (113 ml) bourbon

1 lb (455 g) dark chocolate chips (70-percent dark chocolate chips work great)

2 cups (222 g) cocoa powder

CANDIED PECANS

½ (14-oz [396-g]) can sweetened condensed milk

1 lb (455 g) whole pecans

1 cup (220 g) packed brown sugar

1 tbsp (15 g) salt

In a small saucepan, heat heavy whipping cream with a dash of salt. Bring it to a simmer (or to where it barely begins to steam). You do not want to scald or boil the cream.

Add the bourbon to the hot cream. Turn the heat off. Pour in the dark chocolate chips. Don't stir the mixture; instead, let it sit for about 10 minutes. After sitting for 10 minutes, stir the mixture with a fork and blend until smooth.

Pour the bourbon ganache into a small, deep casserole dish. You want to use a pan that you can easily scoop the bourbon balls out of. Let the ganache sit under refrigeration for about 1 hour or until it's pretty solid. When you'd like to make the bourbon balls, set aside a small, deep dish filled with the cocoa powder. This is what you will roll the balls in to keep them from sticking to one another.

I like to use a 1-ounce (28-g) scoop to form my bourbon balls out of the ganache. I do so by making a long pass with my scoop in the ganache, which will start to form a ball of hardened ganache. Feel free to pack the scoop if you need to in order to achieve that classic round truffle shape. Some chefs even form the balls in their hands after scooping and then toss them in cocoa powder. It's up to you to find your own style in making these.

Preheat the oven to 250°F (121°C).

In a large bowl, mix the condensed milk, pecans, brown sugar and salt until combined. Pour the coated nuts evenly across a silicone-lined baking pan. If you don't have a silicone liner, a piece of parchment paper works great.

Put the pan in the oven and check on the pecans every 10 minutes. I like to take a wooden spoon and stir them on the pan.

Cook the pecans for about 30 minutes total or until they are crispy. Remove them from the oven and allow them to cool completely before you handle them. Store them at room temperature for up to 1 month.

Coat the bourbon balls with candied pecans. They're a nice garnish that complements the flavor of chocolate and bourbon. Refrigerate the bourbon balls in an airtight container for up to 1 week. These make great gifts.

Butcher Babe Tip

I like to use dark chocolate chips for this recipe so I don't have to chop up a ton of chocolate off of a large block. If you don't use dark chocolate chips, that's fine, but you will need to cut the chocolate into fine pieces to make the ganache properly.

FRENCH MACARONS *with* SWISS BUTTERCREAM

There are few recipes that I insist be weighed in grams, but this is one of them. I made this recipe while I represented Rational USA self-cooking centers at the National Restaurant Show in Chicago one year. When I say self-cooking center, I really mean oven. These amazing pieces of kitchen equipment cook food like it was magic. It dosen't hurt to have an amazing recipe for this tricky dessert, either. If you haven't had a French Macaron, let me describe it for you. It's like a chewy almond cookie that fell from heaven. I'm serious. It's light and airy and melts in your mouth. The coveted texture of the macaron's end result is worth every painstaking step. This is the kind of recipe where you HAVE TO FOLLOW THE DIRECTIONS. Pair them with swiss buttercream. Their flavor profiles are as limitless as your imagination. This recipe has only been sucessful with the use of a stand-up mixer.

MAKES 3 DOZEN MACARONS

1¼ cups (125 g) almond flour

1 cup (125 g) powdered sugar

8 oz (225 g) granulated sugar

2½ oz (70 ml) water

6 oz (160 g) egg whites

Gel food coloring (any color), optional

Flavor extract (any flavor), optional

SWISS BUTTERCREAM

2 cups (383 g) granulated sugar

1 cup (237 ml) egg whites, room temperature

1 tbsp (15 ml) lemon juice

2½ cups (574 g) butter, cut into cubes

1 tsp pure vanilla extract, or whatever flavoring you want

Preheat the oven to 325°F (163°C).

Sift the almond flour and powdered sugar into a medium slope-sided stainless steel bowl and set aside.

In a small saucepan over medium-high heat, bring the granulated sugar and water to 235°F (113°C).

In an electric stand mixer with a whisk attachment, beat the egg whites until stiff peaks are reached. (The whites are almost at stiff peaks when they become shiny.) Right before the egg whites are at stiff peaks, slowly pour the cooked sugar down the side of the mixing bowl while the mixer is on high speed.

Remove half of the egg whites and cooked sugar and combine it with the almond flour and powdered sugar. Make a thick paste; do not worry about deflating the egg whites. If you wish to add coloring or flavor extracts, do this now.

Be mindful of scraping the bowl, as little bits of unmixed flour will impede the piping process. Once the paste is nice and smooth, add the remaining half of the egg whites. Now is the time to be conscious of not deflating the egg whites. Use gentle and wide "book folds" to marry the paste and whites until combined. Book folds are created by softly using wide and gentle stirs to incorporate ingredients.

Gently scoop the macaron mixture into a piping bag with a round piping tip (otherwise known as a #12 tip). On a silicon mat or parchment paper, pipe out the macarons, leaving at least 1 inch (2.5 cm) between each cookie. I like to do mine about the size of quarters. After I fill up a tray, I tap it on a flat surface so that they flatten out even more.

Let the macarons set up for at least 10 minutes (or up to 20 minutes) before baking. A slight film needs to form on them so they bake appropriately. Bake for 20 minutes or until you can remove one from the pan.

In the bowl of an electric mixer, add the sugar, egg whites and lemon juice and whisk the mixture over a simmering saucepan of water. Constantly whisk the mixture until the egg whites reach a temperature of 140°F (60°C). Return the bowl to the stand mixture.

(continued)

Beat the egg whites until they form stiff peaks.

Pour in the cooked sugar. This is very difficult without a hand or stand mixer.

Gently add the dry mix into the whipped egg whites.

Gently fold the dry mix into the meringue. Add any food coloring or extracts at this time.

Pipe the mix onto parchment paper or a silpat.

For a traditional macaron, pipe the mixture into the size of a quarter or close to 1 inch (25 mm).

FRENCH MACARONS *with* SWISS BUTTERCREAM *(continued)*

Using the whisk attachment, whisk the sugar–egg white mixture to create stiff peaks. Once you see stiff peaks, switch over to the paddle attachment and start to incorporate the butter on low speed until silky smooth. It might appear that the mixture is breaking, but keep mixing, it will smooth out. Add the vanilla or flavoring of your choice after the butter has been incorporated.

Remove from the mixing bowl and keep at room temperature for up to 48 hours. You can refrigerate the Swiss buttercream for up to 2 weeks. To bring it back to life, add it into the mixer and mix on medium-high speed until smooth.

To assemble these little bites of heaven, carefully pop them off the baking surface. It's very important to do this carefully after they have cooled and become room temperature. Place a nice ribbon of swiss buttercream along the perimeter and place the bottom side of two pieces together. Store at room temperature for up to 48 hours.

DIVINITY MARSHMALLOWS

I feel like Dr. Seuss over here with these fluffy, sweet little things. I could eat them in a car. I could eat them at the bar. I could eat them at the gym. I could eat them with my friends.

Divinity is just that. It's so dang good. This recipe's a little different than any you've probably had, and that's not a bad thing. These are a unique combination of melt-in-your-mouth and chewy all at the same time. It's like a marshmallow and a meringue had a baby.

MAKES 18 (2-INCH [5-CM]) PIECES

4 cups (768 g) granulated sugar

1 cup (240 ml) light corn syrup

¼ cup (60 ml) bourbon

¾ cup (180 ml) water

1 vanilla bean

4 egg whites

1 cup (151 g) roasted pistachios, finely chopped

1 cup (151 g) dried cherries, finely chopped

Butter

2 cups (260 g) powdered sugar

In a medium-size saucepan, combine the granulated sugar, corn syrup, bourbon and water to make a simple syrup. Cook this mixture over medium-high heat to 260°F (127°C). Use a candy thermometer to accurately check the temperature. Scrape the inside of the vanilla bean into the simple syrup.

While the simple syrup is cooking, whip the egg whites to stiff peaks with an electric stand mixer. When the eggs are nice and shiny and hold their shape at stiff peaks, pour the simple syrup into the egg whites on high speed in the mixer. Pour the simple syrup down the side of the bowl, not directly into the whisk.

As soon as the mixture is combined, fold in the toasted pistachios and cherries. Pour this mixture into a dish that's at least 2 inches (5 cm) deep and has been lined with wax paper or coated with butter and powdered sugar. I like to use wax paper. After the divinity has set overnight at room temperature, cut it into 2-inch (5-cm) pieces. Fill a shallow dish with the powdered sugar and roll the divinity marshmallows in the powdered sugar. These make great gifts.

BOURBON CHOCOLATE CAKE

There's something about chocolate cake that makes you make room for dessert. The taller and darker it is, the more seductive.
I'm a huge fan of multilayered cakes. When guests order my cakes by the slice when I'm working at a restaurant, I feel like the pieces
are blowing kisses and hollering, "Hey, y'all" to everyone in the dining room. No joke, a few minutes later,
I start to hear the ticket machine spout off.

SERVES 12

½ lb (228 g) butter, at room temperature, plus more for prepping pans

8 oz (228 g) dark chocolate, melted

4 oz (114 g) sour cream

3 cups (660 g) packed dark brown sugar

8 eggs

2 cups (500 g) flour

1½ cups (167 g) cocoa powder

¼ tsp baking soda

½ cup (120 ml) bourbon

GANACHE

8 oz (240 ml) heavy whipping cream

1 lb (455 g) 70-percent dark chocolate chips

Candied Pecans (page 162), for garnish

Preheat the oven to 325°F (163°C). Prepare 3 (8-inch [20-cm]) circular straight-sided cake pans with parchment paper circles on the bottom of them. Butter the sides of the pans also.

In a medium-size saucepan over medium heat, melt together the dark chocolate and sour cream. Let the chocolate and sour cream cool slightly.

In a stand mixer on medium speed, incorporate the butter and the brown sugar until fluffy. Add the eggs, 2 at a time, and the dark chocolate and sour cream mixture, scraping the sides of the bowl after each addition. In a medium bowl, sift together the flour, cocoa powder and baking soda. With the stand mixer on low speed, add the flour mixture to the mixing bowl in 2 batches, scraping the bowl after each addition.

Divide the batter between the prepared cake pans and bake the cakes for 25 minutes, or until a toothpick inserted in the center of the cakes comes out clean. Let the cakes come to room temperature on the counter top. Cooling the cakes in the fridge will dry them out. Sprinkle the bourbon on the cakes before they are iced with the ganache.

To make the ganache, heat the heavy whipping cream until it starts to steam. Add the chocolate chips to the cream. Let sit for 5 minutes. Stir the mixture with a fork until incorporated.

Continue to temper the chocolate by agitating it until it becomes an icing consistency. Smear a thin layer of ganache on the top of one cake layer, then stack the next layer of cake on top of the iced layer. Repeat this process with the second and third layers of cake. Cover the outside of the cake with a thin layer of ganache as well. Garnish with the Candied Pecans.

PÂTE SUCRÉE

Carbs make me happy. They just make things taste so good in the bake shop! Pâte sucrée is a French-style pastry dough that works for just about everything and it's more on the sweet side. It's a great pie dough to have around. It does great in the freezer for months if you form it into disk shapes and wrap it in butcher's paper. My freezer is full of doughs wrapped in butcher's paper. (Did you know that butcher's paper prevents freezer burn?) Let's make this pie dough to use today, and then some for the freezer.

MAKES 4 (8-INCH [20-CM]) TART BASES OR 3 (8-INCH [2-CM]) PIE DOUGHS OR ABOUT 3 DOZEN COOKIES

5 cups (1.3 kg) pastry flour (in a pinch, all-purpose flour will work fine too)

2 cups (460 g) butter, frozen

4 large egg yolks

6 tbsp (84 g) packed light brown sugar

½ cup (120 ml) heavy whipping cream

Sift the pastry flour into a large bowl. Refrigerate the flour for 30 minutes. Remove the flour from the fridge and, with a potato peeler, fleck pieces of the frozen butter into the flour. I love this trick!

Whisk together the egg yolks, brown sugar and cream in a small measuring cup.

Slowly pour the egg mixture into the flour mixture while gently mixing it in with a wooden spoon. Once the mixture is barely combined, transfer it from the bowl and divide into thirds before placing on a piece of plastic wrap. Let it rest and chill in the fridge for at least an hour before handling. If not using right away, wrap each piece of dough tightly in the plastic wrap before wrapping with butcher's paper. Kept wrapped up tight, this dough will last for months in the freezer.

When you are ready to use the dough, bake it at 350°F (177°C) until golden brown.

PÂTE BRISÉE

When it comes to pastry, pie dough makes the world go round. There are so many kinds. This one in particular is more of a "short dough" variety. It's more neutral as far as flavor goes. It's got a touch of sweet and a touch of salty, but the flavors are ever so subtle. Its buttery flavor has a lot to do with the not-too-traditional addition of lard instead of shortening. This is a great recipe to play around with and make your own.

MAKES 2 (8-INCH [20-CM]) PIE DOUGHS

3 cups (750 g) pastry flour (in a pinch, all-purpose flour will work fine too)

½ tsp salt

1 tsp granulated sugar

6 tbsp (84 g) butter, frozen

¼ cup (55 g) lard

2 tbsp (30 ml) bourbon

2 tbsp (30 ml) water, chilled

Combine the flour, salt and sugar in a large bowl. Fleck in the frozen butter by shaving it with a potato peeler. Add the lard in small pieces by hand.

With a wooden spoon, add the bourbon and water slowly until combined. Divide the dough into 2 equal pieces and place each piece on a large piece of plastic wrap. Form the dough into disks on each piece of plastic, wrap the dough up tightly in the plastic wrap, and put the dough under refrigeration (or in the freezer if you are keeping the dough for a long period of time).

When ready to use the dough, pull a disk out of the freezer and let it rest for at least 30 minutes in the refrigerator. Roll out the dough on a lightly floured surface, until it is about ¼-inch (6-mm) thick, being careful not to overwork it. Bake the dough at 350°F (177°C) until golden brown. When wrapped tightly, this dough lasts for months in the freezer.

APPLE DUMPLINGS

I made apple dumplings for some producers with Food Network a few years ago. These little bites of heaven were my ticket to Food Network Star. My grandma used to make these for me all the time—they are my favorite dessert in the whole world. She used Jonathan apples, a small, red apple known for their sweet flavor. The following recipe is for my grandmother's pie dough, the one she uses when she creates my favorite dessert!

MAKES 8 DUMPLINGS

2 cups (500 g) all-purpose flour, sifted

1 tsp salt

⅔ cup (145 g) shortening

¼ cup (60 ml) cold water

8 apples, peeled and cored (peels reserved)

1 egg yolk

2 tbsp (30 ml) hot water

Coarse sugar, as needed

APPLE FILLING

1 stick butter, cut into 4 pieces (room temperature works best)

3 tbsp (21 g) cinnamon

½ cup (110 g) packed light brown sugar

APPLE DUMPLING SAUCE

Reserved apple peels

2 cups (440 g) packed light brown sugar

½ stick butter

2 bags chai tea

2 cinnamon sticks

1 tsp salt

4 cups (960 ml) water

Preheat the oven to 350°F (177°C). Sift together the flour and salt in a medium bowl. Cut in the shortening and add the cold water to form a ball. Roll the dough out on a floured surface to about ¼-inch (6-mm) thick. Cut out 8 small circles of dough using a pastry cutter or wide glass.

For the apple filling, mix the butter, cinnamon and sugar together until it's a smooth mixture. The mixture should be thick enough to handle.

In a baking dish that's at least 2 inches (5 cm) deep, place a peeled and cored apple in the center of each dough circle. Fill the core of the apple with apple filling, enclosing the apples in pie dough. Mix together egg yolk and hot water until incorporated. Brush all sides of the pie crust with the egg wash and sprinkle with coarse sugar.

Bake the apple dumplings for 35 minutes.

In a medium-size saucepan over medium heat, cook the reserved apple peels, brown sugar, butter, bags of chai tea, cinnamon sticks, salt and water for 30 minutes. The mixture will eventually reduce and create a sticky, candy-like consistency. Remove and discard the tea bags and cinnamon sticks. I like to pour the sauce over the apple dumplings once they are done baking.

If not serving right away, store the sauce separately from the dumplings to prevent the crust from getting soggy. This sauce is good for weeks in the fridge, and also makes a nice addition to any bourbon cocktail.

To bring the apple dumplings back to life, heat them in a 300°F (150°C) oven for 15 to 20 minutes before topping with the sauce.

Surround the apple in the goodness of your pie dough.

Infuse the sauce with whole cinnamon sticks and apple peels.

BROWN BUTTER PEACH CRUMBLE

These crumble-type cakes are fabulous. You can use whatever kind of fruit you want and flavor the crumbles in numerous ways. These crumbles scream for ice cream like a biscuit does butter. There are a lot of ways to make these rustic grandma-style desserts, but I'm going to teach you how my grandma did it.

SERVES 8

1 (8½-oz [241-g]) box white cake mix, such as Jiffy brand

2 cups (480 ml) milk

2 eggs

1 tsp cinnamon

1 stick butter, at room temperature

4 fresh peaches, peeled and pitted

3 tbsp (36 g) coarse sugar

Preheat the oven to 350°F (177°C).

In a medium-size mixing bowl, combine the cake mix, milk, eggs, cinnamon and butter with a whisk and mix until just combined. Pour into a tart pan.

Cut the peaches in half and place them around the pan on top of the cake mix. Sprinkle the coarse sugar on the peaches and bake for 30 minutes. Now you've got a taste of Grandma's house. Where's the ice cream?

AMBROSIA ICE CREAM BARS

Sometimes I think I might have some of the best ideas in the world. This recipe was one of those times. Down in the South, one refreshing dessert reigns supreme. It's ambrosia. Ambrosia is famous for being light and fluffy while being subtly sweet. So I figured why not make it into a popsicle. Err muhhh gawd. Some of the ingredients might seem sort of strange, but trust me!

MAKES 1 DOZEN 4-OUNCE (113-G) POPSICLES

1 (7-oz [198-g]) bag sweetened coconut flakes

1 cup (245 g) vanilla yogurt

2 cups (99 g) small marshmallows

1 stalk celery, small dice

1 orange, segments cut apart and without the rind, or 1 small (8¼-oz [234-g]) can mandarin oranges, drained

1 green apple, unpeeled, small dice

2 cups (360 g) fresh pineapple, small dice

½ cup (50 g) maraschino cherries, drained, small dice

2 cups (480 ml) heavy whipping cream

2 cups (260 g) powdered sugar

Preheat the oven to 275°F (135°C).

Spread the shredded coconut out evenly on a sheet tray. Toast the coconut in the oven for about 10 minutes. Watch closely to ensure it doesn't burn. You want a nice and toasted golden-brown coconut here. Let the coconut cool and set aside.

In a large bowl, mix together the yogurt, marshmallows, celery, orange segments, apple, pineapple and cherries. In a separate large-size bowl, whip the heavy cream to stiff peaks while adding the powdered sugar. Gently fold the whipped cream into the yogurt mixture.

Immediately put this mixture into popsicle molds, place a popsicle stick in the ambrosia and freeze overnight. Once the ambrosia bars are set, I like to remove them from the trays and coat them in the toasted coconut flakes. I keep mine in a large plastic bag or a sealed container; that way, they don't become freezer burnt. Enjoy these frozen treats for up to 30 days.

SMOKED PEACHES 'N' GINGERSNAPS

You can easily do this recipe with any ripe stone fruit. My favorite fruit to use for this is peaches. I love them. Can you tell?

Imagine a gooey, sticky gingersnap that's been cooked on the grill inside an oozing peach . . . Sign me up, 'cause I want two! This recipe is a fun way to start baking on the grill. It's like making an open-faced dessert for a change. There's actually a lot that can be done with an indirect heat source like that. All you need is some confidence and a cast iron. I think they might be the same thing—cast iron equals confidence!

SERVES 8

1 cup (80 g) quick oats

¼ cup (60 ml) bourbon

½ cup (115 g) butter

2 cups (440 g) packed dark brown sugar

2 eggs

2 cups (500 g) flour

1 tsp salt

4 tbsp (28 g) Chinese five-spice powder

¼ cup (60 ml) molasses

1 cup (241 g) candied ginger, cut into small pieces (see Butcher Babe Tip)

4 ripe peaches, peeled and pit removed

Preheat the grill to 400°F (204°C). In a small bowl, soak the oats in the bourbon and set aside. Combine the butter and brown sugar in the bowl of a stand mixer on medium speed until fluffy peaks of butter appear. On medium speed, add the eggs. Scrape the sides of the bowl and then add the flour, salt, Chinese five-spice powder, molasses and candied ginger. Add the butter mixture to the bowl with the bourbon-soaked oats. Let the dough rest for 10 minutes on the counter.

Take a large cast iron skillet and place it in the upper rack of your grill. Let it warm up for about 10 minutes.

In the meantime, fill the peaches with the gingersnap cookie dough. Use the spot where the pit used to be as a well for your cookie dough. Once the peaches are filled, transfer them to the cast iron in the grill, cookie-dough side up.

Turn the grill down to 250°F (121°C) and bake the peaches for 30 minutes. Serve hot. These make great leftovers. Reheat them in the oven for 15 minutes at 350°F (177°C).

Butcher Babe Tip

You can find candied ginger at any specialty grocery store in the spices or baking aisle. It is inexpensive to purchase and is also great in cocktails or tea.

PEPPERMINT CRÈME BRÛLÉE

This crème brûlée is my favorite flavor ever: peppermint! It's the perfect end to a meal. It cleanses your palate in the best way. It's kind of like brushing your teeth, but with a dessert. It also pairs well with bourbon, which is the opposite of brushing your teeth.

SERVES 6-8

8 egg yolks

1 cup (220 g) packed light brown sugar

1 vanilla bean

4 cups (960 ml) heavy cream

1 tsp salt

1 tbsp (15 ml) peppermint extract

Granulated or coarse sugar, as needed

Preheat the oven to 325°F (163°C).

Whisk together the egg yolks and brown sugar in a medium-size bowl. Split the vanilla bean down the center and scrape the insides of the vanilla bean into the egg yolk mixture. Reserve the vanilla bean pod.

In a medium-size saucepan over medium heat, bring the heavy cream to a simmer with the vanilla bean pod. Don't let it boil! Remove the vanilla bean pod from the cream. Slowly pour the hot cream into the egg yolk mixture. Whisk quickly to temper the 2 mixtures together. Add the salt and peppermint extract.

Divide the custard between 6 to 8 ramekins. I like to pour my crème brûlée mix into a pitcher so it's easier to use.

Fill the ramekins up until they are nearly full. Place them in a deep pan, such as a baking dish, and place it in the oven, being careful not to spill. Once the pan is in the oven, slowly pour hot water into the pan from the corner of the dish until the ramekins are at least halfway submerged by water.

Cover the pan with a large piece of foil and bake the crème brûlées for 35 to 45 minutes. They will be done when the center is ever so slightly jiggly. Remove the foil before taking the pan out of the oven; that way, you can see what you're doing. Let the brûlées sit in the water bath for 15 minutes or until they are cool enough to remove from the water bath. Refrigerate them for at least 2 hours.

Once cool, the brûlées are almost ready to serve. Finish the tops with the granulated sugar, add fire to brûlée it. You can use a propane torch to do this, making sure you don't apply the fire to one spot for too long. If you don't have a propane torch, you can use your oven's broiler. Place the sugared brûlées on the top rack of your oven and turn the broiler on high. Watch brûlées carefully, as this only takes 5 to 10 minutes.

Crème brûlée is good for 1 week in the fridge.

Butcher Babe Tips

* I didn't have any ramekins one time, so I used tea cups instead. It actually worked great!

* Add 1 teaspoon of liquid smoke to the mix instead of peppermint for a truly delicious perception changing flavor. If you like toasted marshmallows, you'll love this.

BOURBON-ANA BREAD PUDDING

Nothing says I'm in New Orleans like bananas Foster for dessert, and that's why diners have been doing it for decades. From the chef preparing it tableside to the iconic purple glow as the cinnamon meets the flame midair, it's a gorgeous way to end a meal. I've taken this Southern staple and simplified it a bit. Don't worry—it still packs a punch and is completely suitable for dessert in bed. Never had either? Well, you're in luck. It's a great time to try something new while you try something old.

SERVES 8

1 dozen croissants, cut into ½-inch (13-mm) pieces

5 eggs

3 cups (720 ml) heavy whipping cream

1 cup (220 g) packed brown sugar

½ vanilla bean, scraped, or 1 tbsp (15 ml) vanilla extract

¼ cup (60 ml) bourbon or rum

1 ripe banana

1 tsp salt

1 tsp ground cinnamon

Preheat the oven to 250°F (121°C).

Toast the cut croissants on a baking sheet in the oven until they resemble golden-brown croutons. The drier the bread, the more efficiently it can hold on to the egg mixture, creating a more luscious bread pudding.

Raise the oven temperature to 350°F (177°C).

In a blender, blend the eggs, heavy whipping cream, brown sugar, vanilla bean, bourbon, banana, salt and cinnamon until smooth. It's OK if some small chunks of banana remain. (You can also whisk the ingredients together by hand in a large bowl.)

Put the croissant croutons in a large bowl and pour the custard over them. Let the mixture sit for 15 minutes while slowly agitating to ensure an even distribution of liquid. Transfer the pudding mixture to an oven-safe casserole dish and bake in a water bath (see sidebar) for 45 minutes.

Butcher Babe Tip

A water bath protects egg-infused dishes from getting too hot too quickly. If utilized properly, the end result will be creamy bread pudding. I like to pick out the two dishes I use for this before I begin the recipe so I know I'm set up for success. Basically, one dish needs to fit comfortably inside the other with at least 1 inch (2.5 cm) around the edges as wiggle room. I pull the oven rack out just a bit when I pour the water into the bottom dish. Use hot water, not cold, when pouring around the item to be baked and carefully push the rack back in to the oven.

CHEESECAKE

Everyone thinks they have the best cheesecake recipe.

Whatever. You didn't get yours from a little Swedish man. This somewhat tricky recipe lies within my "too legit to quit" recipe bank. I got it from this cute little old Swedish chef that I used to share a bakery with in Louisville, Kentucky. His attention to detail inspires me today. He had "pastry hands," strong and glowing from all the cocoa butter that laced his works of art. Both beautiful and old, they paid homage to sixty-plus years of hard work.

This man used to collect chocolate "dust" from the workstations of less-than-amateur pastry chefs that had begun internships with us. He would then intimidate the newbies by silently walking around the kitchen and pointing to the several ounces of chocolate dust he had collected. The look on their faces was priceless. I'll never forget all he taught me—including this cheesecake recipe.

MAKES 3 (8-INCH [20-CM]) CHEESECAKES

1½ (6-oz [170-g]) sticks butter, at room temperature

½ cup (65 g) powdered sugar

1½ cups (375 g) all-purpose flour

¼ cup (38 g) cornstarch

1 tsp flavor extract of choice

1 tsp olive oil

3 lb (1.4 kg) cream cheese

1 lb (455 g) granulated sugar

5 large eggs

2 oz (57 g) vanilla malt powder

1 tsp salt

Preheat the oven to 350°F (177°C).

To make the short dough crust, cream together the butter, powdered sugar, flour, cornstarch and flavor extract using a hand or stand mixer on medium speed until well-incorporated. Grease the cake pans with the olive oil and cut out a perfect parchment paper circle to fit the cake pans' bottoms. (By the way, springform pans suck for cheesecake.)

There are two different methods for producing the bottom crust on the cheesecake. Roll the dough out onto a floured surface. It's important to roll the dough out from the middle outwards. I like to roll my dough out to about ½-inch (13-mm) thick and then transfer it to the bottom of the baking pan. It's OK if it rips or tears because you can just apply a little pressure with your fingertips and bring the pieces back together. This method involves then pouring the cheesecake on top of the raw crust and then transferring it to the water bath to bake in the oven.

Or there is option two, where you replicate an exact shape of the cheesecake base, bake it separately then assemble after the bottom of the cheesecake has been cooked and then frozen. This procedure involves a similar process where you will roll out the dough onto a floured surface. I like to roll mine out onto lightly floured parchment paper. I do this for two simple reasons; one, the parchment paper is easy to move from the countertop to the baking sheet, and guess what?!!! No messy countertop to clean. I hate doing dishes.

Bake short dough crust for 15 minutes. Do not turn the oven off.

If you have a stand mixer, outfit it with the paddle attachment. With the mixer on medium-low speed, start to whip the cream cheese. After 5 minutes of mixing, stop once and scrape the bowl. This is the part of the recipe that most people mess up on. The cream cheese actually has to be warm to ensure there will be no lumps.

Prepare a baking sheet by lining it with parchment paper, then bake the granulated sugar for 5 minutes. Remove the sugar from the oven and pour the warm sugar straight into the mixing bowl with the mixer on medium-low speed. After 5 minutes, scrape the bowl.

Put the whole eggs in a medium-size mixing bowl and pour "bath water" temperature water, right from the tap over them so they are submerged. The water temperature should be warm to the touch. After 15 minutes of soaking, they are ready. Remove the eggs from the water, dry them off, and crack them into a medium measuring cup.

Add the vanilla malt powder and salt to the eggs. Whisk the ingredients together with a fork. The eggs will incorporate into the cheesecake batter much better when they are already whipped a bit. Add the egg mixture, one-third at a time, to the batter. Mix for 3 minutes in between every addition of eggs, scraping after every addition.

Pour the cheesecake batter evenly into the prepared cake pans. Lightly tap the pans on the counter as a last attempt to reduce the amount of potential air bubbles.

Place a large, oven-safe pan into the oven. Make sure the cake pans will fit inside whatever vessel you use. I even used a cast iron pan once. Place the cake pans within the large pan. With the oven rack pulled out somewhat, fill the pan carefully with hot water out of the tap. Don't get any water into the batter as you fill the water bath at least halfway up the pans' sides. Slowly push the oven rack back in the oven. Shut the door, bake the cheesecakes for 35 minutes, then give the pans a "jiggle test." You are looking for an "almost set" reaction from the cheesecakes after the jiggle test. Depending on your oven, you may need to turn the pans or cook longer. If the cheesecakes appear to be browning too quickly, cover them loosely with a piece of foil.

When the cheesecakes can pass the jiggle test, remove the pans from the water bath and allow them to cool on cold stovetop burners until they're room temperature, then transfer them to the freezer, covered with plastic wrap. It's best to let the cheesecakes freeze overnight so as to have easy removal from the pan.

Once the cheesecakes are frozen solid, I will quickly set the pans on hot stovetop burners for about 20 seconds at a time.

I gingerly coax the cheesecakes out of their pans while they are upside down with gentle taps. I'll return to warming the cakes' bottoms for intervals until they release. Then I will set them on their short dough crust bases.

Butcher Babe Tip

Making extra cheesecake is not a bad thing! They freeze great. If for whatever reason the cheesecake didn't turn out as planned, it's not a big deal. It goes great in the middle of the Carrot Cake Sandwich Cookies (page 187), or for the gooey centers of the Danish Dough (page 184).

DANISH DOUGH

Do you like flaky layers in your baked goods? This butter-infused dough's got about as many layers as I do and that's a lot. This recipe makes the house smell better than bacon cooking. I said it, and I mean it! The Danish Dough can be made sweet or savory by the various types of fillings you place inside of it. This is a more difficult recipe but it's definitely worth the trouble. By the time you're done rolling it out about 12 times, you'll feel like you've hit the gym. It's nice to justify all the pastries we've eaten somehow.

MAKES 2 DOZEN 3-INCH (7.6-CM) PASTRIES

6 oz (180 g) whole eggs

3 cups (720 ml) whole milk

6 cups (1.6 kg) high-gluten flour

1 cup (192 g) granulated sugar

2 tbsp (30 g) iodized salt

2 tbsp (22 g) instant yeast

3 tbsp (42 g) unsalted butter

Flour, as needed

Olive oil or butter, as needed

1½ lb (683 g) butter block, for lamination

In the large mixing bowl of a stand mixer, combine the eggs, milk, high-gluten flour, sugar, salt, yeast and butter. Mix at low speed for 3 minutes with a dough hook. Remove the dough from the bowl and start to shape it into a rectangle with the help of a little bit of flour on your work surface. When the desired shape of dough is produced, lightly spray it with olive oil or room temperature butter and cover it with plastic wrap. This will protect the dough from creating a skin while it is resting.

Let the dough rest for 20 minutes under refrigeration. While the dough is resting, lay out a full sheet size of parchment paper. This parchment paper will act as a vessel for a butter block. This layer of butter is the basis for the beautiful flaky layers that make a Danish dough so unforgettable.

I like to use a rolling pin to evenly distribute the butter in the parchment paper pouch. As you will soon discover, there is a fine line between smashing the butter on the paper and bursting the paper open. I feel as though it's easier to distribute the butter when it's room temperature and then refrigerate it. I chill mine until it's solid, and then I lay it down onto the dough.

After the dough has doubled in size, punch it down to release any bubbles and then let it rest on a floured surface in the fridge for about 30 minutes so that no skin can form. I take this opportunity to start to shape it into a rectangle that is about 1-inch (25-mm) thick, or a 12-inch (30-cm) square.

Once the dough has rested, it's time to start to laminate the dough with the butter, ultimately creating the beautiful flaky layers. Cut the dough and the butter in half, into two equally sized pieces. Roll the dough out into rectangles that are about 18 x 8 inches (45 x 20 cm). The pieces should 'match' the butter layer that you've created separately. Set aside.

Lay the butter piece over one layer of dough and then put the second piece of dough over that. You're kind of making two butter sandwiches at this point. Seal the edges with your fingertips by applying pressure to the edges all the way around.

Place the two butter sandwiches on top of one another.

Preheat the oven to 325°F (163°C). Refrigerate your dough for at least 30 minutes.

After 30 minutes, fold the dough into thirds again and roll out into an 18 x 8-inch (45 x 20-cm) rectangle. Refrigerate for an additional 30 minutes. Fold the dough again, roll out to an 18 x 8-inch (45 x 20-cm) rectangle and cut into 3 x 3-inch (8 x 8-cm) squares. Place onto a lined baking sheet and let the dough rise until it has increased in size by ⅓. Bake immediately for 15 to 20 minutes until golden brown.

PÂTE À CHOUX

With just one recipe, you can make a plethora of mouthwatering bites! I'm talking about éclairs, cream puffs, profiteroles and doughnuts over here. This dough bakes up into a golden crispy crust, leaving its interior virtually hollow after being piped out and baked in the oven. The void left behind within the finished product just begs for some sort of delicious filling. You can go sweet or savory with these things, just like the Danish Dough.

MAKES 4 DOZEN BITE-SIZE CREAM PUFFS

1 cup (240 ml) water

3 tbsp (36 g) granulated sugar

¾ cup (188 g) all-purpose flour

½ tsp salt

½ cup (120 g) unsalted butter, at room temperature

9 oz (250 g) eggs

Powdered sugar, optional

Preheat the oven to 350°F (177°C). In a heavy-bottomed saucepan over medium heat, combine the water, sugar, flour, salt and butter with a wooden spoon. Continue to incorporate for about 5 minutes as the panada becomes a thick paste.

Cook this mixture on the stovetop until the bottom of the pan has a nice and even coat of the panada itself. The development of this layer of film signifies it's time to transfer the panada to a mixer and incorporate the eggs.

Using a stand mixer equipped with a paddle attachment on high speed, start whipping the panada. This part of the process cools the mixture so that you can add the eggs. As a general rule, I know when it's time to add the eggs once I can comfortably leave my hands touching the bowl. Add the eggs 1 at a time.

Take the mixture and place it in a pastry bag. Make nice little mounds of dough on top of a large baking sheet. Place them in the oven and bake for 15 minutes. Then turn the oven down to 275°F (135°C) for an additional 35 minutes or until the dough is dried out.

You can use this same mixture and turn it into Beignets (page 192).

Using the same pastry bag, squeeze the Pâte À Choux in a medium to large-size saucepan of fryer oil that's been heated to 350°F (177°C). Remove from the oil once it becomes a nice golden brown. Serve immediately with powdered sugar.

Butcher Babe Tip

These last forever in the freezer in an airtight container or plastic bag. By forever I mean up to 6 months. Discard if freezer burn occurs.

Cooking the Pâte À Choux on the stovetop.

The perfectly cooked Pâte À Choux. Notice its shiny texture.

CARROT CAKE SANDWICH COOKIES

In 2016, I was working at the National Restaurant Show in Chicago when this dessert accidentally came to be. Chef Thomas Keller was speaking on behalf of Rational Self-Cooking Center while I executed the desserts for up to five thousand people in four days. I had plenty of oatmeal cookies on hand and extra cheesecake. So, these two things plus shredded carrots equaled Carrot Cake Sandwich Cookies. The cheesecake stood in the place of the more traditional cream cheese icing that carrot cake is famous for. #duh.

MAKES 1 DOZEN COOKIES

1 cup (230 g) butter, at room temperature

1 cup (220 g) packed light or dark brown sugar

1½ cups (375 g) all-purpose flour

1 tsp baking soda

2 large eggs

½ cup (58 g) chopped toasted walnuts

3 cups (241 g) old-fashioned rolled oats

2 tbsp (30 ml) bourbon

1 tbsp (7 g) ground cinnamon

1 cup (151 g) raisins

1½ cups (511 g) packed shredded carrots

¼ cup (60 ml) honey

½ tsp salt

CREAM CHEESE ICING

8 oz (288 g) cream cheese, softened

2 cups (130 g) sifted powdered sugar

1 tsp vanilla

Cream the butter and brown sugar with a hand or stand mixer at medium speed for about 5 minutes until fluffy. Add the flour and baking soda to the butter mixture until barely combined. The rest of this recipe you will finish by hand with a wooden spoon or spatula while you combine the toasted walnuts and oats. Set aside.

In a small saucepan over medium heat, combine the bourbon, cinnamon, raisins, carrots, honey and salt. Cook for about 10 minutes. Be careful to stir often to prevent burning. Let the mixture return to room temperature, then add it to the cookie base. Mix until combined on low speed.

Refrigerate the cookie dough for at least 1 hour. Preheat the oven to 325°F (163°C). Scoop out desired cookie size and bake on a large baking sheet until desired doneness. I like mine a little chewy, so I bake mine for 10 minutes in a 2-ounce (56-g) portion size.

To make the cream cheese icing, combine the cream cheese with the powdered sugar and vanilla in a medium bowl using an electric hand mixer. This icing stays fresh under refrigeration for up to 1 week.

Let the cookies cool and make sandwich cookies by putting the cream cheese icing between 2 cookies (alternatively, you can fill them with the Cheesecake [page 182]).

SHORT DOUGH SUGAR COOKIES *with* ROYAL ICING

This recipe melts in your mouth. Mostly because all the butter makes me feel that way. This dough is heavenly, easy to make and has a nice sweet and salty balance. Sometimes I pretend that the cookie does melt in my mouth—along with the calories. I invite you to do the same.

MAKES 2 DOZEN 2-INCH (5-CM) COOKIES

1½ cups (195 g) sifted powdered sugar

1 cup (230 g) softened butter

1 egg

1 tsp vanilla extract

2½ cups (625 g) sifted all-purpose flour

1 tsp baking soda

1 tsp cream of tartar

ROYAL ICING

4 cups (520 g) sifted powdered sugar

2 egg whites

Juice of 1 lemon

Dash water, if needed

Food coloring, as needed

With a hand or stand mixer, cream together the powdered sugar and butter. Add the egg and vanilla. Add the flour, baking soda and cream of tartar. Let the dough chill in the fridge for 2 hours.

Preheat the oven to 375°F (191°C). Roll the dough out into the desired shapes or put it into a cookie press. Keep the dough less than ½-inch (13-mm) thick, but no less than ¼-inch (6-mm). Bake the cookies for 10 minutes or until slightly golden brown.

To make the royal icing, combine the powdered sugar, egg whites, lemon juice, water (if needed) and food coloring in a large mixing bowl using a whisk. Pour the icing over the baked cookies or use a piping bag to create intricate designs on the cookies. Let the iced cookies set for 30 minutes before handling.

Store baked cookies for weeks in an airtight bag. The dough lasts for months in the freezer.

SEVEN LAYER BARS

These disappear. For real. My grandma made these for me all the time while I was growing up. I loved coming home from school and having these sweet treats to enjoy—they are almost as sweet as her. I said almost.

SERVES 8

6 tbsp (84 g) butter, melted

1½ cups (241 g) crushed vanilla wafers

1 cup (180 g) chocolate chips

1 cup (180 g) toffee chips or butterscotch chips

1 cup (76 g) sweetened shredded coconut

1 (14-oz [233-ml]) can sweetened condensed milk

Preheat the oven to 325°F (163°C).

Pat down the butter and crushed vanilla wafers in the bottom of an 8 x 8-inch (20 cm x 20-cm) baking dish.

On top of the crust, make layers of the ingredients, starting with the chocolate chips, toffee chips and shredded coconut, then pour the sweetened condensed milk over the top.

Bake the layered mixture for 20 to 25 minutes. Let it cool to room temperature. Cut the layers into bars. Watch them disappear. I would tell you how long they last out in the open, but they won't last that long. You can hide them in the freezer for a few months.

BEIGNETS WITH BOURBON DIPPING SAUCE

My earliest memories of growing up in Louisiana revolve around bakeries. I can remember not being tall enough to see over the counter to watch the crispy beignets dance in the fryer oil. The coolest part of waiting for my hot and sugary treat was that once I had a basket of donuts in my hand it felt like Christmas morning. I would hold my mouth open like a baby bird letting the powdered sugar from the air sail straight into my mouth while the chef was finishing this iconic Southern staple.

The truth is people like donuts everywhere, probably even on the moon.

I made a version of this dish the time I won *Cutthroat Kitchen*. Oh and don't forget the bourbon, I didn't!

SERVES 8

Pâte à Choux dough (page 185)

Powdered sugar, as needed

BOURBON DIPPING SAUCE

¼ cup (60 ml) maple syrup

2 tbsp (30 ml) bourbon

2 tbsp (28 g) packed brown sugar

¼ cup (36 g) fresh corn kernels

1 tbsp (15 ml) heavy whipping cream

Using the same pastry bag from the Pâte à Choux recipe, squeeze the dough in a medium to large-size pan of fryer oil that's been heated to 350°F (177°C). Remove the Beignets from the oil once they become a nice golden brown. Serve them immediately with powdered sugar sprinkled on top or dipped in the Bourbon Dipping Sauce. Taste the South, y'all.

To make the Bourbon Dipping Sauce, bring the maple syrup, bourbon, brown sugar and corn to a boil in a small saucepan. Add the heavy whipping cream and remove the saucepan from the heat. Serve with the Beignets on the side. Yes!

VITAMIN C MERINGUE PIE

This pie is a crowd-pleaser. It tastes like lemonade. It's refreshing and it's got lemons in it so it must be good for you, right? It packs a punch and is pretty easy to make. My grandma used to make them all the time in the winter when there was snow on the ground, because she said that it "tasted like summertime."

SERVES 6

1 premade pie shell, or recipe from Pâte Sucrée (page 170), chilled

⅓ cup (50 g) cornstarch

2 cups (383 g) granulated sugar

1½ cups (355 ml) lemonade (store-bought is fine)

6 egg yolks

3 tbsp (43 g) butter

Zest of 4 large lemons or oranges (reserve juice in place of the lemonade if you wish)

½ cup (118 ml) lemon juice, fresh is best

MERINGUE

4 egg whites, room temperature

¼ cup (32 g) powdered sugar

Preheat oven to 350°F (177°C). Make sure the pie dough is chilled in the freezer for a few minutes before baking in the oven. Par bake the pie shell in the oven for 7 to 8 minutes or until slightly browned. Let cool on the counter top.

In a 2-quart (2-L) saucepan over medium heat, mix the cornstarch and sugar in with the lemonade, stirring constantly, until the mixture thickens and boils.

Whisk in the egg yolks and cook for an additional 2 minutes on medium heat. Be careful not to let the bottom burn. Remove from the heat and add the butter, citrus zest and lemon juice. Pour into the pie crust.

In a medium bowl, beat the egg whites on high speed until foamy. Mix in the powdered sugar slowly then beat until you reach stiff peaks. Stiff peaks are nice and shiny and keep their shape when touched. Spread the whipped egg whites over the hot pie filling to the very edges of the pie dough.

Bake around 10 minutes until the meringue is light brown. Keep an eye on it in the oven. Remove the pie from the oven and cool for 2 hours until cold. A clean rack in the fridge is a great place. Store in the refrigerator. Pie is best if eaten within 48 hours. Yum!

Crimp the edges of the pie dough. Egg wash evenly and sprinkle with sugar.

Dock the raw pie dough with a fork to create little holes in the dough, before it par bakes.

Dollop the stiff egg whites over the cooked lemon mixture. We want height here!

Chapter 8

BE STILL AND GLOW, THERE'S BOURBON:
~ Drinks ~

I love bourbon. It's good hot or cold and anywhere in between. There's no occasion I can think of where bourbon can't be enjoyed. Or a dish that bourbon can't elevate.

I fell in love with the romanticized tradition of bourbon once I moved to Louisville, Kentucky, when I worked in a bourbon-themed French bistro–style restaurant.

Once I learned how to pronounce "Louisville" with a true Kentucky drawl, it only seemed natural that I learned how to enjoy a nice glass of bourbon too. So that's exactly what I did.

The following bourbon-laced cocktails are my favorite ways to enjoy bourbon.

Cheers!

LEMONADE TEA

I love to play off the classics. There's something so refreshing about lemonade and bourbon. If you don't believe me, then ask all the whiskey sour lovers out there.

This crowd-pleaser cocktail is easy to make for one or for a crowd. I haven't met a person who can't enjoy at least one of these. This recipe is also great if you need some vitamin C.

Add some sunshine and enjoy.

Bourbon: Angel's Envy
Flavor Profile: Bright and sunny
Pair it With: Sixty-Minute Carnitas (page 53), Steak Tartare (page 48) and Shrimp Cocktail (page 125)

MAKES 2 TALL COCKTAILS

4 cups (960 ml) water

3 bags tea (I recommend mint-infused black tea)

2 cups (440 g) packed light brown sugar

Pinch salt

4 cups (560 g) ice, plus more for serving

8 oz (240 ml) bourbon

Fresh mint leaves, plus more for garnish

Juice of 6 lemons

On the stovetop in a saucepan, combine the water, tea bags, brown sugar and salt. Bring to a boil for about 5 minutes, until all the brown sugar is dissolved and the tea bags have steeped. Remove the saucepan from the heat.

Add the ice and let the mixture chill. Remove the tea bags from the liquid. Next, add the bourbon, mint and lemon juice.

Fill 2 large mason jars with additional ice and pour the Lemonade Tea in the glasses. Garnish with a few more sprigs of mint.

WATERMELON GRIND

So maybe you've never made it to the Kentucky Derby. That's fine. This bourbon-infused popsicle will make you feel like you have. It's like a healthy drink from a juice bar, but with bourbon in it.

Bourbon: Maker's Mark
Flavor Profile: Fruity and sweet with a crisp, refreshing finish
Pair it With: Cheat day during your new diet or a backyard barbecue

MAKES 1 DOZEN 4-OUNCE (113-G) POPSICLES

1 package watermelon flavor gelatin

2 cups (480 ml) bourbon, at room temperature

1 small seedless watermelon

Fresh mint leaves

Dissolve the package of watermelon gelatin in the bourbon. Set aside.

Peel the skin off the watermelon and cut in half. Reserve the watermelon's flesh. Cut the watermelon rind into chunks and toss them in a food processor with the reserved watermelon flesh and a handful of mint until about ¼-inch (6-mm) pieces are achieved.

Combine the gelatin mixture with the watermelon puree until incorporated and pour the liquid into popsicle molds. Add popsicle sticks a few hours later (this way, they will stick in the center of the frozen treat). Allow the popsicles to freeze overnight.

If you want to speed up the process, it's easy to use an ice cube tray. Let the cubes set up for at least 2 hours in the freezer.

COMING UP ROSES

A couple days of the year, there are roses everywhere in Kentucky. I mean everywhere. The botanical fragrance of roses also belongs in a showstopping cocktail, not just on derby hats.

Besides the unmistakable flavor of rose petals being an interesting ingredient, I also like to use Tellicherry peppercorns (also known as pink peppercorns), which are the seeds of a relative of the rose bush. Their fiery pop of feminine sweetness is always a pleasant surprise.

Bourbon: Four Roses
Flavor Profile: For the adventurous palate
Pair it With: Wedding dress shopping

MAKES 4 COCKTAILS

2½ cups (600 ml) water, divided

4 tbsp (56 g) packed light brown sugar

1 tsp red chili flakes

1 tsp Tellicherry peppercorns

Zest of 2 oranges

2 cups (280 g) ice, divided

Juice of 2 oranges

4 tsp (120 ml) grenadine

8 oz (240 ml) bourbon

In a saucepan over high heat, cook ½ cup (120 ml) of the water, the brown sugar, red chili flakes and peppercorns for about 5 minutes. Bring this mixture to a simmer until a simple syrup starts to form. Stir frequently.

Remove the saucepan from the heat and allow the syrup to cool until slightly warm. At this point, add the orange zest and pour the simple syrup into a French press. Add 1 cup (140 g) of the ice and the remaining 2 cups (480 ml) of water on top of the simple syrup, along with the orange juice.

Agitate the cocktail with the French press until a froth begins to form.

Fill 2 tall glasses half full with the remaining 1 cup (140 g) of ice and divide the grenadine and bourbon between them. Pour the rose cocktail mixture right out of the French press over the ice and take a seat. No need to run around anymore—you're coming up roses.

AFFOGATO WHERE MY KEYS ARE

A full belly can give you a case of food coma. I'm sure everyone can attest to that. It's customary at that point for a nice cup of coffee to be consumed and put some pep back in your step . . . Especially with some bourbon in it. This delightfully thoughtful coffee cocktail will get your feet back on the floor running. It's kind of like an Irish coffee but different—a reinvented digestif that remembers you still wanted dessert. That's why there's ice cream in it. I love you.

Bourbon: Wild Turkey

Flavor Profile: Coffee and a hug

Pair it With: Late night at the office or a nice end to a wonderful dinner;
goes especially great with the Vitamin C Meringue Pie (page 195)

MAKES 4 SMALL COCKTAILS

½ cup (110 g) packed brown sugar

Ice, as needed

½ cup (120 ml) heavy whipping cream

16 oz (480 ml) cold-brew coffee

8 oz (240 ml) bourbon

1 pint (483 g) vanilla ice cream

Divide the brown sugar between 2 mason jars. Fill the mason jars with ice until they are three-fourths full.

Gently pour the heavy whipping cream between the 2 glasses, trying not to disturb the brown sugar.

Divide the coffee between the 2 glasses, top each with 4 ounces (120 ml) of bourbon and a big dollop of vanilla ice cream.

You're gonna need a straw. And place to sit down for a while.

MELON BALLER

In the South, we eat a ton of melons. Luckily, they start popping out and bursting with refreshing juice during the hottest part of the year. At times they are so plentiful that we have to start finding creative ways to use them before they "get away from us." So, why not drink them? With bourbon!

Bourbon: Bulleit Rye
Flavor Profile: Light and refreshing, like a summer breeze
Pair it With: Anything barbecued, fresh seafood and salads

MAKES 4 COCKTAILS

1 large cantaloupe or honeydew melon

4 cups (560 g) ice

Juice of 2 limes (rinds reserved)

4 oz (113 g) fresh ginger, peeled

4 oz (120 ml) honey or agave nectar

1 cup (240 ml) bourbon

Crystallized honey, for serving

Clean and peel the melon, removing any seeds and being careful to keep the juice for the cocktail. Cut the melon into wedges small enough to fit in a blender. In the blender, combine the ice, lime juice, ginger, honey, bourbon and melon. Blend on high until smooth.

With reserved lime rind, wet the rims of 4 glasses and rim them with the crystalized honey. Serve with a straw.

STRAWBERRY RHUBARB ICE BAR

This bourbon-laced icy treat tastes like the month of May, when all those beautiful ingredients you've been dreaming about all winter start to come to life all over again. May is the month when all the veggies and fruits start to spring up and remind us that summer is in full swing. After the addition of bourbon, you can even taste the hint of a bonfire. Hello, summertime. We missed you.

Bourbon: Jim Beam Black
Flavor Profile: Sweet and tangy, refreshing and relaxing
Pair it With: Friends who are new to drinking bourbon; goes great with appetizers and salads

MAKES 4 COCKTAILS

2½ cups (600 ml) water

1 cup finely minced rhubarb

1 package strawberry flavor gelatin

Juice of 2 lemons

Zest of 2 lemons

¼ cup (38 g) thinly sliced fresh strawberries

⅓ cup (80 ml) bourbon

In a saucepan, combine the water and rhubarb.

Bring this mixture to a boil for 5 minutes. Remove the saucepan from the heat and stir in the strawberry gelatin. Then add the lemon juice and lemon zest. If you add the zest too early in the cooking process, it has the tendency to become bitter and lose its bright flavor as the oils leach out.

Next, add the sliced strawberries. Pour the bourbon into the mixture and you're almost done. Pour the mixture into popsicle molds and freeze for 8 to 12 hours. An hour or so after putting the popsicle molds in the freezer, place the popsicle sticks in the center of the popsicles. That way, they can be frozen in the center. Enjoy.

Butcher Babe Tip

Never use the leaves of the rhubarb plant (or rhubarb in its raw state for that matter), because they contain oxalic acid, which can be poisonous in large doses.

GONZO

Hunter S. Thompson was a character. He was also a Louisville, Kentucky native. His request for his ashes
to be shot out of a cannon over Cherokee Park after his death was fulfilled. This cocktail is to celebrate his life until his death.
He had to go out with a bang, just like this cocktail.

Bourbon: Angel's Envy
Flavor Profile: Like you're on an island writing a book
Pair it With: Filing your taxes

MAKES 2 COCKTAILS

FALERNUM SYRUP

3 lb (1.4 kg) fresh ginger, peeled and cut into 1-inch (2.5-cm) pieces

Juice of 3 lb (1.4 kg) limes

1 lb (455 g) granulated sugar

4 oz (118 ml) bourbon, divided

Crushed ice, as needed

1 oz (28 ml) freshly squeezed lime juice

Coconut water, as needed

Fresh star fruit, as needed

Orange bitters, as needed

In a saucepan, cook the ginger, lime juice and sugar until the syrup reaches 240°F (116°C) on a candy thermometer.

Fill a glass half full with crushed ice. Add half of the bourbon. Combine 3 ounces (85 ml) Falernum syrup with 1 ounce (28 ml) of lime juice. Fill the remainder of the glass with coconut water and a dash of orange bitters. Serve with a few slices of star fruit.

OLD BUICK WITH KENTUCKY PLATES

I've driven across the country twice in my 1991 Buick LeSabre. This car floated over Route 66 and never missed a beat. I bought the car from my Great-Aunt Juanita, who purchased it brand new over two decades ago. I remember riding in the car as a little girl, thinking it was the fanciest car I'd ever ridden in. It only seemed fair that I name a cocktail after my car. I love her. She has baby blue velour interior and a matching paint job. Don't forget about the whitewall tires and the spoked rims. They don't make things like they used to. This punch is pretty good, though, and you can make it yourself.

Bourbon: Blanton's
Flavor Profile: Fruity, refreshing, fun
Pair it With: Any get together with several people; Smokey Root Beer Pork Butt (page 54) and Swine Apple (page 58)

SERVES 12

1 package orange flavor gelatin

Maraschino cherries, as needed

1 quart (965 g) citrus sherbet

½ bag mini marshmallows

8 cups (1.9 L) citrus soda

4 cups (960 ml) bourbon

Make a frozen ring mold with the orange gelatin and maraschino cherries. In a punch bowl, combine the sherbet, marshmallows, soda and bourbon. Serve and enjoy!

ACKNOWLEDGMENTS

THANK YOU TO:

Page Street Publishing

Alton Brown

Albert W. A. Schmid

L.E. Kincaid & Sons Butchershop

Michael Crouch

Steven Sarro

Kristi Sparks

Chelsea Butler

Elizabeth Seise

The Gavin Family

Jessica Ebelhar

Anne Neese

Lana Del Rey

Isaac Brock

Hugh Acheson

Maneet Chauhan

Bettie Page

ABOUT THE AUTHOR

Loreal first appeared on national television as a contestant on *The Next Food Network Star*. During that competition, she became best known as The Butcher Babe™. Loreal went on to win an episode of the Food Network's *Cutthroat Kitchen*. She has also been seen on Rachael Ray. She was featured as a celebrity chef at The Fantastic Food Fest, a culinary celebration in Indianapolis, Indiana.

Loreal has extensive experience in the food industry, including working at L.E. Kincaid & Sons Butcher Shop in Indianapolis for 4 years. She holds an associate degree of culinary arts from Sullivan University in Louisville, Kentucky. She spent half a decade living and working in Louisville, Kentucky cooking for various distillers at the restaurant Bourbons Bistro. She has worn many hats in the hospitality industry. She has been a culinary school instructor, pastry chef, hospitality consultant, butcher and private chef.

Loreal was born in Lafayette, Louisiana and moved to Indiana when she was eight years old. She currently resides in Louisville, Kentucky. She is planting roots in the blue grass state, where she is developing her own line of textiles. The hospitality industry–inspired wares will be reminiscent of her own personal art work.

INDEX